Xuan Kong Nine Life Star

六白金星命

Six White Life Star

Feng Shui Essentials: Xuan Kong Nine Life Star
SIX WHITE LIFE STAR

Copyright © 2011 by Joey Yap
All rights reserved worldwide.
Second Edition January 2013

All intellectual property rights contained or in relation to this book belongs to Joey Yap.

No part of this book may be copied, used, subsumed, or exploited in fact, field of thought or general idea, by any other authors or persons, or be stored in a retrieval system, transmitted or reproduced in any way, including but not limited to digital copying and printing in any form whatsoever worldwide without the prior agreement and written permission of the author.

The author can be reached at:

Mastery Academy of Chinese Metaphysics Sdn. Bhd. (611143-A)
19-3, The Boulevard, Mid Valley City,
59200 Kuala Lumpur, Malaysia.
Tel   : +603-2284 8080
Fax   : +603-2284 1218
Website : www.masteryacademy.com

DISCLAIMER:

The author, Joey Yap and the publisher, JY Books Sdn Bhd, have made their best efforts to produce this high quality, informative and helpful book. They have verified the technical accuracy of the information and contents of this book. Any information pertaining to the events, occurrences, dates and other details relating to the person or persons, dead or alive, and to the companies have been verified to the best of their abilities based on information obtained or extracted from various websites, newspaper clippings and other public media. However, they make no representation or warranties of any kind with regard to the contents of this book and accept no liability of any kind for any losses or damages caused or alleged to be caused directly or indirectly from using the information contained herein.

Published by JY Books Sdn. Bhd. (659134-T)

Table of content :

1	**LIFE STAR REFERENCE TABLE**	7
2	**INTRODUCTION**	12
3	**YOUR XUAN KONG LIFE STAR**	23
	Basic Attributes	24
4	**YOUR FENG SHUI ESSENTIALS**	27
	Directions	29
	Taking the Direction using a Compass	33
	Favorable Directions	39
	Unfavorable Directions	49
	Bed Alignment Direction	58
	Best Floor	60
	Personal Grand Duke Direction	65
	Personal Clash Direction	71
	Flying Star Effects	76
5	**THE FIVE ELEMENT**	97

6	**CHARACTERISTICS OF STAR**	109
	The Good	111
	The Bad	117
7	**CAREER AND WEALTH**	123
	Characteristics at work	124
	Suitable Job Roles	128
	Career and Wealth Guide	132
8	**RELATIONSHIPS**	139
	Guide for Relationships	140
9	**HEALTH**	145
	Guide for Health	146
10	**COMPATIBILITY with OTHER LIFE STARS**	151

LIFE STAR REFERENCE TABLE

Year Pillar and Gua Number Reference Table for 1912 - 2055

Animal	Year of Birth			Gua Number for Male	Gua Number for Female	Year of Birth			Gua Number for Male	Gua Number for Female
Rat	1912	壬子 Ren Zi	Water Rat	7	8	1936	丙子 Bing Zi	Fire Rat	1	5
Ox	1913	癸丑 Gui Chou	Water Ox	6	9	1937	丁丑 Ding Chou	Fire Ox	9	6
Tiger	1914	甲寅 Jia Yin	Wood Tiger	5	1	1938	戊寅 Wu Yin	Earth Tiger	8	7
Rabbit	1915	乙卯 Yi Mao	Wood Rabbit	4	2	1939	己卯 Ji Mao	Earth Rabbit	7	8
Dragon	1916	丙辰 Bing Chen	Fire Dragon	3	3	1940	庚辰 Geng Chen	Metal Dragon	6	9
Snake	1917	丁巳 Ding Si	Fire Snake	2	4	1941	辛巳 Xin Si	Metal Snake	5	1
Horse	1918	戊午 Wu Wu	Earth Horse	1	5	1942	壬午 Ren Wu	Water Horse	4	2
Goat	1919	己未 Ji Wei	Earth Goat	9	6	1943	癸未 Gui Wei	Water Goat	3	3
Monkey	1920	庚申 Geng Shen	Metal Monkey	8	7	1944	甲申 Jia Shen	Wood Monkey	2	4
Rooster	1921	辛酉 Xin You	Metal Rooster	7	8	1945	乙酉 Yi You	Wood Rooster	1	5
Dog	1922	壬戌 Ren Xu	Water Dog	6	9	1946	丙戌 Bing Xu	Fire Dog	9	6
Pig	1923	癸亥 Gui Hai	Water Pig	5	1	1947	丁亥 Ding Hai	Fire Pig	8	7
Rat	1924	甲子 Jia Zi	Wood Rat	4	2	1948	戊子 Wu Zi	Earth Rat	7	8
Ox	1925	乙丑 Yi Chou	Wood Ox	3	3	1949	己丑 Ji Chou	Earth Ox	6	9
Tiger	1926	丙寅 Bing Yin	Fire Tiger	2	4	1950	庚寅 Geng Yin	Metal Tiger	5	1
Rabbit	1927	丁卯 Ding Mao	Fire Rabbit	1	5	1951	辛卯 Xin Mao	Metal Rabbit	4	2
Dragon	1928	戊辰 Wu Chen	Earth Dragon	9	6	1952	壬辰 Ren Chen	Water Dragon	3	3
Snake	1929	己巳 Ji Si	Earth Snake	8	7	1953	癸巳 Gui Si	Water Snake	2	4
Horse	1930	庚午 Geng Wu	Metal Horse	7	8	1954	甲午 Jia Wu	Wood Horse	1	5
Goat	1931	辛未 Xin Wei	Metal Goat	6	9	1955	乙未 Yi Wei	Wood Goat	9	6
Monkey	1932	壬申 Ren Shen	Water Monkey	5	1	1956	丙申 Bing Shen	Fire Monkey	8	7
Rooster	1933	癸酉 Gui You	Water Rooster	4	2	1957	丁酉 Ding You	Fire Rooster	7	8
Dog	1934	甲戌 Jia Xu	Wood Dog	3	3	1958	戊戌 Wu Xu	Earth Dog	6	9
Pig	1935	乙亥 Yi Hai	Wood Pig	2	4	1959	己亥 Ji Hai	Earth Pig	5	1

- Please note that the date for the Chinese Solar Year starts on Feb 4. This means that if you were born in Feb 2 of 2002, you belong to the previous year 2001.

Year Pillar and Gua Number Reference Table for 1912 - 2055

Animal	Year of Birth			Gua Number for		Year of Birth			Gua Number for	
				Male	Female				Male	Female
Rat	1960	庚子 Geng Zi	Metal Rat	4	2	1984	甲子 Jia Zi	Wood Rat	7	8
Ox	1961	辛丑 Xin Chou	Metal Ox	3	3	1985	乙丑 Yi Chou	Wood Ox	6	9
Tiger	1962	壬寅 Ren Yin	Water Tiger	2	4	1986	丙寅 Bing Yin	Fire Tiger	5	1
Rabbit	1963	癸卯 Gui Mao	Water Rabbit	1	5	1987	丁卯 Ding Mao	Fire Rabbit	4	2
Dragon	1964	甲辰 Jia Chen	Wood Dragon	9	6	1988	戊辰 Wu Chen	Earth Dragon	3	3
Snake	1965	乙巳 Yi Si	Wood Snake	8	7	1989	己巳 Ji Si	Earth Snake	2	4
Horse	1966	丙午 Bing Wu	Fire Horse	7	8	1990	庚午 Geng Wu	Metal Horse	1	5
Goat	1967	丁未 Ding Wei	Fire Goat	6	9	1991	辛未 Xin Wei	Metal Goat	9	6
Monkey	1968	戊申 Wu Shen	Earth Monkey	5	1	1992	壬申 Ren Shen	Water Monkey	8	7
Rooster	1969	己酉 Ji You	Earth Rooster	4	2	1993	癸酉 Gui You	Water Rooster	7	8
Dog	1970	庚戌 Geng Xu	Metal Dog	3	3	1994	甲戌 Jia Xu	Wood Dog	6	9
Pig	1971	辛亥 Xin Hai	Metal Pig	2	4	1995	乙亥 Yi Hai	Wood Pig	5	1
Rat	1972	壬子 Ren Zi	Water Rat	1	5	1996	丙子 Bing Zi	Fire Rat	4	2
Ox	1973	癸丑 Gui Chou	Water Ox	9	6	1997	丁丑 Ding Chou	Fire Ox	3	3
Tiger	1974	甲寅 Jia Yin	Wood Tiger	8	7	1998	戊寅 Wu Yin	Earth Tiger	2	4
Rabbit	1975	乙卯 Yi Mao	Wood Rabbit	7	8	1999	己卯 Ji Mao	Earth Rabbit	1	5
Dragon	1976	丙辰 Bing Chen	Fire Dragon	6	9	2000	庚辰 Geng Chen	Metal Dragon	9	6
Snake	1977	丁巳 Ding Si	Fire Snake	5	1	2001	辛巳 Xin Si	Metal Snake	8	7
Horse	1978	戊午 Wu Wu	Earth Horse	4	2	2002	壬午 Ren Wu	Water Horse	7	8
Goat	1979	己未 Ji Wei	Earth Goat	3	3	2003	癸未 Gui Wei	Water Goat	6	9
Monkey	1980	庚申 Geng Shen	Metal Monkey	2	4	2004	甲申 Jia Shen	Wood Monkey	5	1
Rooster	1981	辛酉 Xin You	Metal Rooster	1	5	2005	乙酉 Yi You	Wood Rooster	4	2
Dog	1982	壬戌 Ren Xu	Water Dog	9	6	2006	丙戌 Bing Xu	Fire Dog	3	3
Pig	1983	癸亥 Gui Hai	Water Pig	8	7	2007	丁亥 Ding Hai	Fire Pig	2	4

- Please note that the date for the Chinese Solar Year starts on Feb 4. This means that if you were born in Feb 2 of 2002, you belong to the previous year 2001.

Year Pillar and Gua Number Reference Table for 1912 - 2055

Animal	Year of Birth			Gua Number for Male	Gua Number for Female	Year of Birth			Gua Number for Male	Gua Number for Female
Rat	2008	戊子 Wu Zi	Earth Rat	1	5	2032	壬子 Ren Zi	Water Rat	4	2
Ox	2009	己丑 Ji Chou	Earth Ox	9	6	2033	癸丑 Gui Chou	Water Ox	3	3
Tiger	2010	庚寅 Geng Yin	Metal Tiger	8	7	2034	甲寅 Jia Yin	Wood Tiger	2	4
Rabbit	2011	辛卯 Xin Mao	Metal Rabbit	7	8	2035	乙卯 Yi Mao	Wood Rabbit	1	5
Dragon	2012	壬辰 Ren Chen	Water Dragon	6	9	2036	丙辰 Bing Chen	Fire Dragon	9	6
Snake	2013	癸巳 Gui Si	Water Snake	5	1	2037	丁巳 Ding Si	Fire Snake	8	7
Horse	2014	甲午 Jia Wu	Wood Horse	4	2	2038	戊午 Wu Wu	Earth Horse	7	8
Goat	2015	乙未 Yi Wei	Wood Goat	3	3	2039	己未 Ji Wei	Earth Goat	6	9
Monkey	2016	丙申 Bing Shen	Fire Monkey	2	4	2040	庚申 Geng Shen	Metal Monkey	5	1
Rooster	2017	丁酉 Ding You	Fire Rooster	1	5	2041	辛酉 Xin You	Metal Rooster	4	2
Dog	2018	戊戌 Wu Xu	Earth Dog	9	6	2042	壬戌 Ren Xu	Water Dog	3	3
Pig	2019	己亥 Ji Hai	Earth Pig	8	7	2043	癸亥 Gui Hai	Water Pig	2	4
Rat	2020	庚子 Geng Zi	Metal Rat	7	8	2044	甲子 Jia Zi	Wood Rat	1	5
Ox	2021	辛丑 Xin Chou	Metal Ox	6	9	2045	乙丑 Yi Chou	Wood Ox	9	6
Tiger	2022	壬寅 Ren Yin	Water Tiger	5	1	2046	丙寅 Bing Yin	Fire Tiger	8	7
Rabbit	2023	癸卯 Gui Mao	Water Rabbit	4	2	2047	丁卯 Ding Mao	Fire Rabbit	7	8
Dragon	2024	甲辰 Jia Chen	Wood Dragon	3	3	2048	戊辰 Wu Chen	Earth Dragon	6	9
Snake	2025	乙巳 Yi Si	Wood Snake	2	4	2049	己巳 Ji Si	Earth Snake	5	1
Horse	2026	丙午 Bing Wu	Fire Horse	1	5	2050	庚午 Geng Wu	Metal Horse	4	2
Goat	2027	丁未 Ding Wei	Fire Goat	9	6	2051	辛未 Xin Wei	Metal Goat	3	3
Monkey	2028	戊申 Wu Shen	Earth Monkey	8	7	2052	壬申 Ren Shen	Water Monkey	2	4
Rooster	2029	己酉 Ji You	Earth Rooster	7	8	2053	癸酉 Gui You	Water Rooster	1	5
Dog	2030	庚戌 Geng Xu	Metal Dog	6	9	2054	甲戌 Jia Xu	Wood Dog	9	6
Pig	2031	辛亥 Xin Hai	Metal Pig	5	1	2055	乙亥 Yi Hai	Wood Pig	8	7

- Please note that the date for the Chinese Solar Year starts on Feb 4. This means that if you were born in Feb 2 of 2002, you belong to the previous year 2001.

To download your Six White Life Star Reference Chart FREE go to

www.masteryacademy.com/regbook

Here is your unique code for access:

GBSN6016

Introduction

When all is said and done, Feng Shui is the study of how environments affect the people living within them. It can yield advice on which environments, at both a macro and micro level, are 'good' places or 'bad' places to live for given people at given times.

Xuan Kong is only one subsection of the study of Feng Shui and the Life Stars are only one component in the Xuan Kong Feng Shui system. This means that the study of Life Stars gives us only one piece of the overall Feng Shui puzzle but it is an important one!

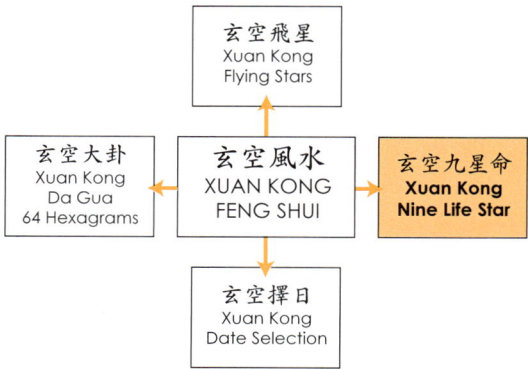

We can use the Xuan Kong Life Star system to help us with a number of practical Feng Shui and interpersonal decisions that make a big impact.

When we assess Feng Shui we assess four factors: Environment, Buildings, Time and People. This book has been written to complement a number of other Feng Shui titles;

1. *Feng Shui for Homebuyers – Exterior;*
2. *Feng Shui for Homebuyers – Interior;*
3. *Feng Shui for Apartment Buyers; and*
4. *Pure Feng Shui.*

These other books talk about the influence of Environment, Buildings and Time on Feng Shui. This book looks at the final aspect: **People.**

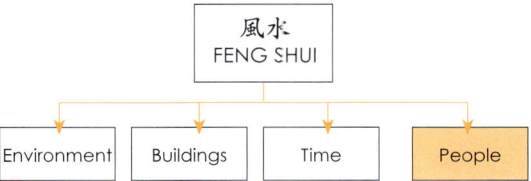

Different people will be affected in different ways by any given environment. The Life Stars directly determine what role the environment plays in the lives of its occupants. Every person is governed by one of the 9 Life Stars. These Stars also help determine key personal characteristics.

In this book, you will learn how the annually changing Xuan Kong Flying Stars interact with your Life Star so that you know what different sectors of your home will bring you. You can then use this information for your own benefit and safety. For maximum benefit, people should seek to align themselves with the direction in their home that yields positive effects. For instance, the #9 Purple Flying Star brings about the potential of career advancement for Star 1 people. Clearly this is a benefit that professionally minded people would like to take advantage of, so they may wish to spend more time absorbing the influence of the #9 Purple Flying Star in their home or place of work. The same Flying Star also indicates a heightened risk of miscarriage for pregnant women though and so pregnant Life Star 1 women should be exercise heightened caution in the presence of this Flying Star, and avoid its influence if possible.

Because the advice generated by this book on Xuan Kong Life Stars takes into account your Life Star when discussing the effects of the Flying Stars, the advice given is highly tailored to your life.

The Positive Side Of You

Your Life Star brings a force to bear on you, wherever you are. This force can have positive or negative effects, depending on the Feng Shui of the environment you reside in.

We are all multi faceted and complex. We have good habits and bad habits; a strong side and a weak side. By correctly tapping into the right Qi your best side will manifest itself more. When you put your best foot forward more in life, more opportunities

and success comes your way. Conversely, if you find yourself under the negative influence of your Life Star, more of your negative personality traits will prevail. Your environment filters out the good or the bad influence of your Life Star. Xuan Kong Feng Shui shows us how we can align ourself to receive the best possible influence. By simply aligning your bed and study desk to correspond with your favourable Personal Directions for example, you can already take one big step towards absorbing the beneficial influence of your Life Star, even whilst you sleep and study! If you are choosing a new home then choosing the correct floor at the correct time will bring further benefits. Avoiding your Personal Grand Duke and Crash Sectors will keep health problems and conflict at bay.

Does all of this mean you must tip-toe around certain rooms in your house or seal them off? No. Feng Shui does not need to become all consuming. If you can easily align your bed so that you receive benefits then why not do so? There are real world limits to what can be done, it is not practical, for instance, to rebuild your home if it does not perfectly cater to the instructions that this book gives. Your ideal floor choice in a condominium may not be available. The list of real world complications goes on.

You can tailor Feng Shui to work for you; making smaller, simple changes so that you reap the maximum possible benefit. The pursuit of good Feng Shui is not intended to take up all of your time and this flexible book is perfect for anyone, no matter how busy or restricted you are in your decisions.

Your Life Star

Everyone falls under the jurisdiction of one of the 9 Life Stars and this will have different consequences for everyone. Your Life Star describes your key skills, characteristics and traits. Some people are creative but reserved, some people are aggressive and driven. What self destructive traits do you have? Do you have a bloated sense of pride or are you prone to gossip? Your Life Star can shine some light on the complexity of your personality and your good and bad traits.

Study of the Life Stars has practical benefits for everyone; it gives you valuable information about others in addition to yourself. Different Life Stars bestow different abilities on people which means that people belonging to each Star will exhibit different characteristics at work. A Star 1 person is diplomatic so they are best suited to roles demanding diplomacy, for example. Accordingly, employers can study the Xuan Kong Life Stars when making work place decisions whilst employees can use the system to help them go about working productively with their colleagues and superiors, even when disagreements arise.

If you become aware of your own harmful tendencies then you can learn to minimize them so you can advance. Similar benefits can be seen in romantic relationships and friendships. Learning that a Star

7 individual needs their space and independence might help you accommodate this in your dealings with them when you might otherwise have been tempted to be clingy and dependant.

When we understand more about ourselves we can stop ourselves from making mistakes and perhaps forgive certain behaviour in others once we understand where it comes from.

Compatibility Guide

Certain people are, of course, more compatible with each other than others. In partnerships or relationships this takes on a new level of importance. Different Life Stars bestow the qualities of different elements on different people; for example, a Star 1 person has the qualities of water whilst a Star 7 person has the qualities of the Yin Metal element. Just as the elements control, pacify and weaken one another, individuals of the different Stars may dominate, clash with or enrich one another. This book includes a write up of how compatible different Stars are with one another. You may find that a relationship as a Star 1 person with a Star 5 person simply isn't worth the effort. A compatibility guide on each interaction gives you tips on how to best deal with the other Stars for mutual benefit, even taking into account your differences.

Compatible With BaZi Profiling Systems

If you are familiar with the **BaZi Profiling System** then you will be aware that, at first glance, it seems to deal with very similar issues. It can tell us about other preferences and internal view of the world. Do we have an optimistic view of things? Do we blame ourselves too much?

While there is some overlap between the jurisdiction of the Xuan Kong Life Star system and BaZi Profiling System, they are two different systems. They both deal with individual people and their personalities but they are not mutually exclusive. In fact, when studied together, they can be thought of as two pieces of the same puzzle.

The BaZi Profiling System tells us about ourselves and about others. It even tells us things that cannot be observed about others (things people do not communicate). What it can't tell us is how the outside environment plays into the picture. The Xuan Kong Nine Stars help determine *which* qualities are brought out and by what features and external forms in the environment.

Once we know what directions are conducive to good Qi, how external forms (pylons etc) can compound problems related to sectors in the home, which areas of our environment increase the risk of which ailments or even which people can create problems in our lives (compatibility guide) then we can begin shaping our external environment to whatever degree necessary in order to enjoy the most happiness, wealth and success. Xuan

Kong Feng Shui tells you precisely what effect the environment and compass directions will have on which people.

If you are simply interested in learning what makes a person tick rather than making decisions about an ideal environment for them to thrive in then I recommend you take up further study of the BaZi Profiling System. The goal of BaZi is to pinpoint personal deficiencies so that they may be overcome or to highlight personal strengths so that they may be capitalised on.

If you are trying to configure your environment in order to maximize the benefits that your home or place of work bestow upon you in terms of health, wealth and relationships, then the Feng Shui Xuan Kong Life Star system is the one for you.

When you combine the two systems and employ them on yourself you will be able to make the most of your best qualities and then seek out an environment which lets you shine and gives the least resistance. A powerful combination of self improvement and informed decision making!

An Easier Life

Life doesn't have to be difficult. It is possible to effectively dodge conflict, problem situations and health problems if you know they are coming. The Life Stars hold the key to many of the "surprises" that life has in store for us and we can learn to shape our environment to our own advantage. This is exciting stuff! Seeking out the best romantic relationships and business opportunities is a top priority for most people and the power of your Life Star can be called upon in these pursuits.

Even though much is made of the layout of the home with relation to Feng Shui, you won't need to bend over backwards to accommodate the advice given in this book. For instance, where you cannot choose the ideal living floor specified, second and third choices are mentioned. You can take as much or as little from this book as you need without fear of it making you paranoid and prey to "paralysis by analysis". Looking back on your own life, you can most probably think of two or three big mistakes – a bad business deal or choice in romantic partner, perhaps. Avoiding pitfalls of this magnitude in the future is made a whole lot easier when you have some idea of how likely they are to occur. If you can make changes to your environment to further reduce this likelihood then all the better!

I hope that this book expands your world view. Once you know how to utilize them, the Nine Stars can be the harbinger of great fortune instead of misery for you. If you can stay on the 'correct side' of your Star and always position yourself to bask in its positive influence then many happy successes await you.

Joey Yap
July, 2011

 www.facebook.com/joeyyapFB

Author's personal website :
www.joeyyap.com

Academy websites :
www.masteryacademy.com | www.maelearning.com |
www.baziprofiling.com

六白金星命

Six White Life Star

Life Star 6	Born in
Male	1931, 1940, 1949, 1958, 1967 1976, 1985, 1994, 2003, 2012
Female	1928, 1937, 1946, 1955, 1964 1973, 1982, 1991, 2000, 2009

- Please note that the date for the Chinese Solar Year starts on Feb 4. This means that if you were born in Feb 2 of 2002, you belong to the previous year 2001.

Your Xuan Kong Life Star

Your Xuan Kong Life Star is Gua #6, and your trigram is called Qian. It looks like this:

For the rest of this book, we will refer to your Gua #6 as Life Star 6.

Basic Attributes of Star 6

Your Life Star 6 is of the Yang Metal element, and such shares some of the traits of Metal when it manifests its Yang qualities. Yang Metal is associated with the sword and the axe, and the colors that are linked to it are grey and blue. You represent the 'King' or the emperor, and your Life Star embodies prestige, justice and authority. Your style is not so much to do the work as to be the arbiter of morals and law instead. You are skilled at delegating the work to others and roles which allow you to do this are the most suitable.

As a Life Star 6, you are known for being upright and diligent. You tend to command respect easily from others, and this seems to work in your favor because you have the responsibility and mandate to go with the power that you wield. You tend to go by the book in what you do, and as such others feel that they can trust you to be in charge of a situation.

At the same time, relying too much on the book can make you rigid, inflexible, and lacking in imagination. You are a stickler for rules, which can sometimes be a problem as some laws are bad and some rules are meant to be broken! You can have too much pride, and may have difficulty getting started on anything until you are pushed or prodded by others.

Basic Emotions & Temperament

Plus : Righteousness, organized, loyal, efficient, perseverant

Minus: Depressive, controlling, demanding, stubborn, opinionated

方向

YOUR FENG SHUI ESSENTIALS

The Feng Shui Essentials comprise Feng Shui Directions, the effects of the Xuan Kong Nine Stars in various sectors and areas of your home and workspace, and the Five Elements.

Each of these factors interact with your Life Star in different ways that will affect how your Life Star manifests itself and determine whether or not it brings out good or bad qualities in you.

Directions

Directions

Direction is an integral component of understanding Xuan Kong Nine Life Stars. Different directions in your home and your place of work can either accentuate or depreciate the strength of your Life Star.

Favorable Direction will highlight or enhance the positive traits of your Life Star, while an Unfavorable Direction will diminish or weaken your Life Star and bring out some of its negative attributes.

The Life Star numbers are categorized into two groups: the East Group and the West Group. The names 'East Group' and 'West Group' are just to demarcate the Greater and Lesser Yin transformation of the Tai Ji. They do not literally represent directions.

East Group Life Stars include 1, 3, 4 and 9. Those who are Life Stars 2, 6, 7 and 8 belong to the West Group. The following table will give you a quick reference of the Auspicious and Inauspicious compass directions of the East and West Group.

East Group 東命

卦 Gua	生氣 Shen Qi Life Generating	天醫 Tian Yi Heavenly Doctor	延年 Yan Nian Longevity	伏位 Fu Wei Stability	禍害 Huo Hai Mishaps	五鬼 Wu Gui Five Ghosts	六煞 Liu Sha Six Killings	絕命 Jue Ming Life Threatening
坎 Kan 1 Water	東南 South East	東 East	南 South	北 North	西 West	東北 North East	西北 North West	西南 South West
震 Zhen 3 Wood	南 South	北 North	東南 South East	東 East	西南 South West	西北 North West	東北 North East	西 West
巽 Xun 4 Wood	北 North	南 South	東 East	東南 South East	西北 North West	西南 South West	西 West	東北 North East
離 Li 9 Fire	東 East	東南 South East	北 North	南 South	東北 North East	西 West	西南 South West	西北 North West

West Group 西命

卦 Gua	生氣 Shen Qi Life Generating	天醫 Tian Yi Heavenly Doctor	延年 Yan Nian Longevity	伏位 Fu Wei Stability	禍害 Huo Hai Mishaps	五鬼 Wu Gui Five Ghosts	六煞 Liu Sha Six Killings	絕命 Jue Ming Life Threatening
坤 Kun 2 Earth	東北 North East	西 West	西北 North West	西南 South West	東 East	東南 South East	南 South	北 North
▶ 乾 Qian 6 Metal	西 West	東北 North East	西南 South West	西北 North West	東南 South East	東 East	北 North	南 South
兌 Dui 7 Metal	西北 North West	西南 South West	東北 North East	西 West	北 North	南 South	東南 South East	東 East
艮 Gen 8 Earth	西南 South West	西北 North West	西 West	東北 North East	南 South	北 North	東 East	東南 South East

The concepts of Favorable and Unfavorable are derived from the Eight Wandering Stars system of the Ba Zhai Eight Mansion Feng Shui 八宅風水.

Each of the 8 directions is governed by a Star. These Wandering Stars will affect each Xuan Kong Life Star in different ways. Each Life Star has four Favorable Directions governed by Auspicious Stars: Sheng Qi 生氣 (Life Generating), Tian Yi 天醫 (Heavenly Doctor), Yan Nian 延年 (Longevity), and Fu Wei 伏位 (Stability).

The four Unfavorable Directions are governed by Inauspicious Stars and include Huo Hai 禍害 (Mishaps), Wu Gui 五鬼 (Five Ghost), Liu Sha 六煞 (Six Killings) and Jue Ming 絕命 (Life Diminishing).

The following diagram shows you the Favorable and Unfavorable Directions for Star 6.

Taking the Direction using a Compass

You will need a compass – or alternatively, the Joey Yap iLuoPan app for iPhone available at the Apple App Store – to determine the direction of your Main Door, Bed and Stove. Hold your compass or iLuoPan at waist level as shown on the illustration below. Your compass or iLuoPan will align to the magnetic North on its own. All you need to know is how to take your direction as indicated on the following pages.

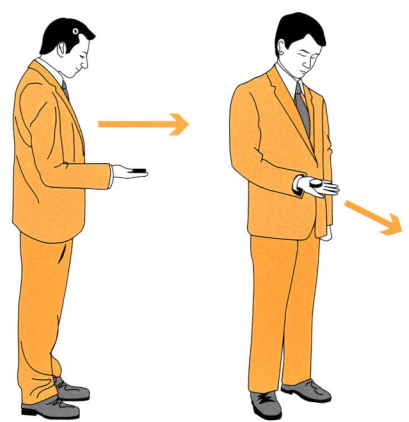

Facing Direction of the Main Door

1. Stand about one foot outside the door looking outwards.

2. Use the square base of your compass to help you align yourself parallel to the door.

3. Read the facing direction on your compass.

Facing Direction of the Bed

1. Measure from the head of the bed where your head is placed when you lie down (the direction the headboard faces) and not the direction your feet face.

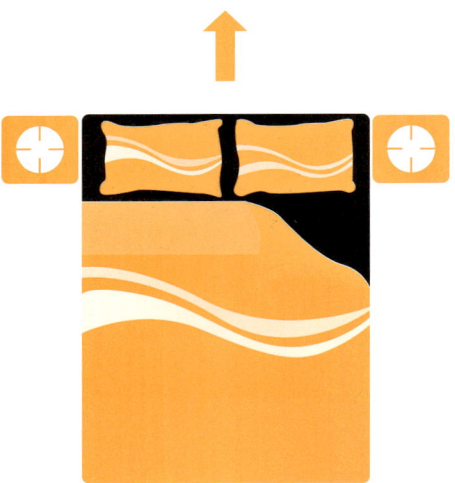

Facing Direction of the Stove

1. For modern (gas or electric) stoves, look at the where direction of the cooking knobs (fire igniters) are pointing to determine its facing direction.

2. For traditional stoves that require wood and fire to work, look for their 'fire mouth' as the facing direction.

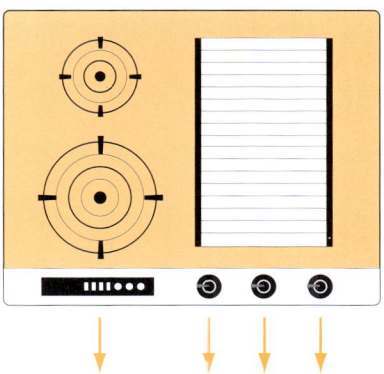

Favorable Directions

West
西 (262.6°-277.5°)

Life Generating
生氣 (Sheng Qi)

The basic characteristics of the Sheng Qi Star:

It brings about promotions, career advancements, strong money and wealth luck, potential political power and authority, and all-round success.

The Sheng Qi Star represents life-generating Qi or energy. It also represents the Wood Element, and hence, governs the facets of success, authority, nobility, status and wealth in life. Wood relates to growth and advancement in life, and as such is an extremely auspicious Star to tap into. For you, the West direction taps into the Sheng Qi potential.

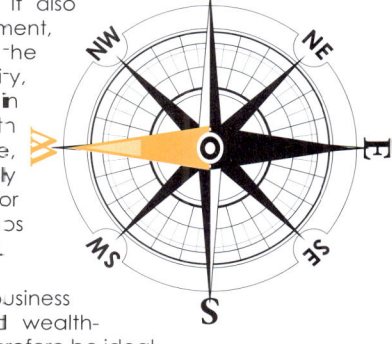

This Star is suitable for business (commercial), career and wealth-related pursuits. It would therefore be ideal for a business or residence to have its Main Door situated in the Sheng Qi sector as it allows you to tap into these energies to create opportunities for profit and long term wealth opportunities.

Sheng Qi is an active star by nature and thus, it is not conducive for rest or sleep-related activities. It is best to avoid having the bed or bedroom located in this sector or for anyone to sleep facing this direction. Use this sector for your work or for active pursuits instead of relaxing ones.

If this sector is missing from a house or is lacking in the office or the premises of a business, the wealth-related aspects of your career or venture will be considerably weakened and it will be a difficult struggle to amass wealth and prosperity.

Northeast
東北 (37.6°-52.5°)

Heavenly Doctor
天醫 *(Tian Yi)*

The basic characteristics of the Tian Yi Star:

It brings about general good luck and well-being, as well as positive mentor luck or the presence of sound advisors and guidance.

This Star represents the Earth Element and is therefore the determinant of noble people (mentors) and people of caliber and status. It also denotes your health prospects and physical wellbeing. As such, the Tian Yi Star is best utilized to help generate guidance for your career or for any project which you've embarked upon. It will bring about the help and assistance of others.

It is also a useful Star for health purposes, and its benefits can be employed when you need to recuperate, recover, or heal from an illness, surgical procedure or health issue.

When the Tian Yin sector is missing from a home or office, your health is likely to suffer because of it. In addition, you will also find help from noble people hard to come by, especially in times of need in life and career matters. You will come across more obstacles and obstructions which you must overcome on your own without the external help of others.

Since the Tian Yi Star represents nobility, it also governs your reputation, respectability, and your oratory powers. It thus has influence on your powers of speech and persuasion, and has some bearing on how you are perceived by others and how well they respond to your verbal overtures.

Southwest
西南 (217.6°-232.5°)

Longevity
延年 *(Yan Nian)*

The basic characteristics of the Yan Nian Star:

It prolongs and enhances life and improves the quality of your life. It promotes good communication with others which in turn makes for good relationships.

The Yan Nian Star represents the Metal Element, and as such governs speech and the effectiveness of your words. If you are looking to establish good relationships and rapport with others, you will need the help of this Star, since it governs aspects of successful networking, communication and relationship building.

The Yan Nian Star is important for family harmony and domestic bliss. It is also necessary if you wish to build good relationships with co-workers and colleagues. Essentially, it paves the way for smooth interpersonal relations, seldom plagued by misunderstanding, arguments and flare-ups. As such, the presence of the Yan Nian Star is useful for maintaining harmony.

If you are employed in public relations or marketing and you must interact with clients and customers as part of your daily routine, you will find the Qi brought about by this Star very useful to your career.

Do note that if the Yan Nian sector is missing, harmony and unity will be adversely affected, and relations are likely to be tense or strained. At the very least, you can expect more argument and discord with others.

Northwest
西北 (307.6°-322.5°)

Stability
伏位 (Fu Wei)

The basic characteristics of the Fu Wei Star:

It is a Star that promotes calm and keeps you grounded. It allows for peace of mind and rationality. It also promotes good luck.

The Fu Wei Star represents the Wood Element. When qualities or virtues such as calmness and tranquility are required, this is the Star you need! It promotes peace of mind and heightens clarity of thought, so this is also the Star to use if you need to focus, study or make important decisions.

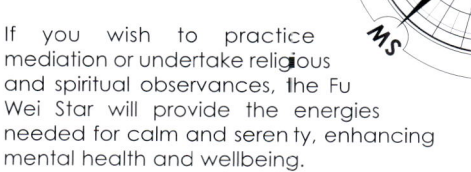

If you wish to practice mediation or undertake religious and spiritual observances, the Fu Wei Star will provide the energies needed for calm and serenity, enhancing mental health and wellbeing.

This Star is most suitably applied to libraries, study areas/zones or other places where concentration is necessary. When considering the home or workplace, this Star can help create areas where the mind can be easily quietened and people can reflect and turn inward.

When the Fu Wei sector is missing from a place, peace of mind will be difficult to attain.

Unfavorable Directions

Southeast
東南 (127.6°-142.5°)

Mishaps
禍害 (Huo Hai)

The basic characteristics of the Huo Hai Star: It denotes potential calamities, accidents, and mishaps. It undermines good efforts and brings about the risk of mistakes and errors.

The Huo Hai Star represents the Earth Element and is the harbinger of mishaps, loss of wealth, sudden (unfortunate) changes or hassles as well as work-related obstacles. What it does is undermine your efforts and bring about sudden obstructions or problems that will result in a loss of time and energy.

If, for example, the Main Door of a property is located in this direction, you can reasonably expect to encounter quite a few obstacles and problems in your daily life. It is best to work around this area particularly if your main door or office is located in the West sector.

The detrimental effects of a negative star are compounded when it is located within an area that is already affected by negative Feng Shui, so pay attention to the negative structures outside this area.

East
東 (82.6°-97.5°)

Five Ghosts
五鬼 (Wu Gui)

The basic characteristics of the Wu Gui Star:

It brings about betrayal and treachery through back-stabbing, gossip, and rumors. It also denotes endless bickering and fraught tension brought about by arguments.

The Wu Gui Star represents the Fire Element and is the bringer of betrayal, ill-intentioned gossip, rumours, backstabbing, cruelty, petty people and even subterfuge and sabotage. It generally denotes a sense of unease brought upon by less-than-honest speech.

The presence of Wu Gui in a house causes disloyalty and discord amongst family members, affecting relationships and marriages. If it is present in your work place, then you should also watch out for fights and arguments between your colleagues or subordinates and friction or tension with your superiors.

Negative external forms such as (sharp) pylons and jagged rooftops pointing towards a house further aggravate the effects of this Star.

North
北 (352.6°-7.5°)

Six Killings
六煞 (Liu Sha)

The basic characteristics of the Liu Sha Star:

This Star brings about injuries and accidents. It also denotes the possibility of betrayals and dishonesty, and the risk of potential scandals.

The Liu Sha Star relates to the element of Water and is the harbinger of lawsuits and potential scandals. Legal problems at the workplace or adulterous affairs in relation to your marriage or personal relationships could be brought to light.

This Star is also the harbinger of bodily injury, harm and conditions requiring people to undergo physical surgery. Robberies and theft are also likely, and you will have to be careful about what information you share with others and with the general safety of your personal documents and possessions.

Be mindful of the presence of negative external forms, which will compound the adverse effects of this Star. For instance, a Y-shaped road at the Liu Sha sector will result in scandalous affairs, while negative structures as mentioned earlier will compound and exacerbate the harmful effects of the Liu Sha Star.

South

南 (172.6°-187.5°)

Life Threatening
絕命 *(Jue Ming)*

The basic characteristics of the Jue Ming Star:

It brings about the risk of accidents and major illness, and the threat of miscarriage for pregnant women. It also signals potential for great calamity.

This Star represents the Metal Element and it signifies accidents and illnesses. The energies of the Jue Ming Star are quite severe and so are its adverse effects, bringing with it considerable risk.

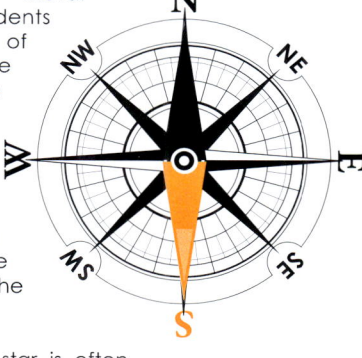

In severe cases, the Jue Ming Star can even cause fatal accidents, ailments or injuries when there are negative external forms outside of the South sector.

It is to no surprise that this star is often regarded as the primary star of misfortune and calamity in the study of Ba Zhai Feng Shui. Other than catastrophes and accidents, it can also cause major loss of wealth and theft as well as the cause of breakups or separation in relationships.

Bed Alignment Direction

One of the key Feng Shui factors of the bedroom is how your bed is placed. For starters, your bed should preferably be pushed against a wall, with the headboard also against it. The most important thing you can do when laying out your bedroom with regards to Feng Shui is to make sure your headboard is aligned with your Favorable Direction.

Facing Direction, in the case of bed alignment, refers to the direction of your headboard. This means it is the direction your head faces when you lie down on the bed, and **not** the direction that your feet face.

As a Star 6, your Bed Alignment Directions are:

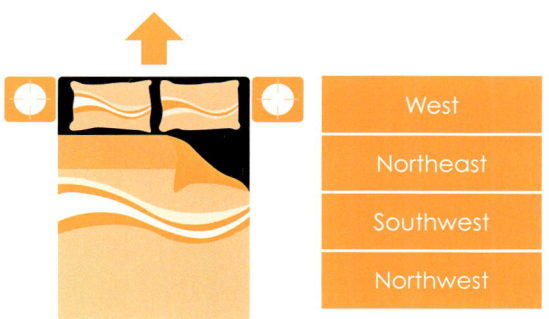

West

Northeast

Southwest

Northwest

Best Floor

A reality of modern life is that most of us do not live in houses these days, instead living in multi story apartments and condominium blocks.

Some of us are pretty mobile and live a nomad-like lifestyle that may require us to stay in high-rise buildings for certain periods of time. As such, it becomes important to select the right floor to reside in. The objective of this is to achieve elemental affinity between you (the occupant) with the energies of a particular floor.

As you are a Star 6 person of the Metal element, the chart below gives you the best floors for you to live on in terms of first choice, second choice, and third choice.

First Choice	Second Choice	Third Choice
4th Floor	5th Floor	3rd Floor
9th Floor	10th Floor	8th Floor
14th Floor	15th Floor	13th Floor
19th Floor	20th Floor	18th Floor
24th Floor	25th Floor	23rd Floor
29th Floor	30th Floor	28th Floor
34th Floor	35th Floor	33rd Floor
39th Floor	40th Floor	38th Floor
44th Floor	45th Floor	43rd Floor
49th Floor	50th Floor	48th Floor

Select :
Earth shaped buildings & Metal shaped buildings

Avoid :
Fire shaped buildings & Water shaped buildings

Personal Grand Duke Directions

Identifying the Grand Duke Sector is important. Your Personal Grand Duke Sector relates to your birth year. For example, if you are born in the year of the Rat then the Rat is your Personal Grand Duke and we know that the Rat sector is North 2.

We want to avoid the harmful properties of this area and as you are a Star 6 person, you can locate your Personal Grand Duke Sector in the following directions:

Personal Grand Duke Directions for Male

MALE Birth Year	Personal Grand Duke	Direction
1913, 1949, 1985, 2021	丑 Chou Ox	東北 1 **Northeast 1**
1922, 1958, 1994, 2030	戌 Xu Dog	西北 1 **Northwest 1**
1931, 1967, 2003, 2039	未 Wei Goat	西南 1 **Southwest 1**
1940, 1976, 2012, 2048	辰 Chen Dragon	東南 1 **Southeast 1**

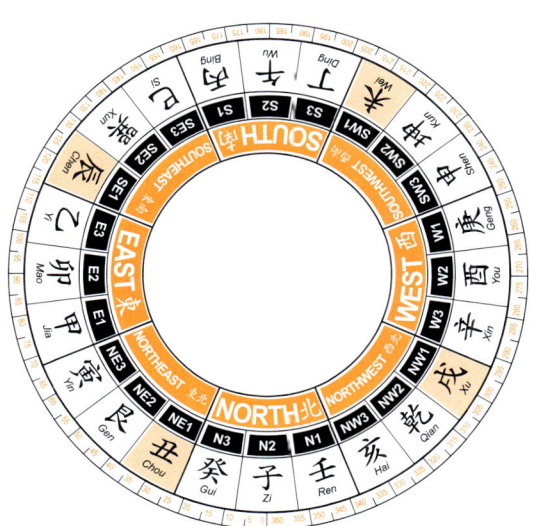

Personal Grand Duke Directions for Female

FEMALE Birth Year	Personal Grand Duke	Direction
1919, 1955, 1991, 2027	未 *Wei* Goat	西南1 Southwest 1
1928, 1964, 2000, 2036	辰 *Chen* Dragon	東南1 Southeast 1
1937, 1973, 2009, 2045	丑 *Chou* Ox	東北1 Northeast 1
1946, 1982, 2018, 2054	戌 *Xu* Dog	西北1 Northwest 1

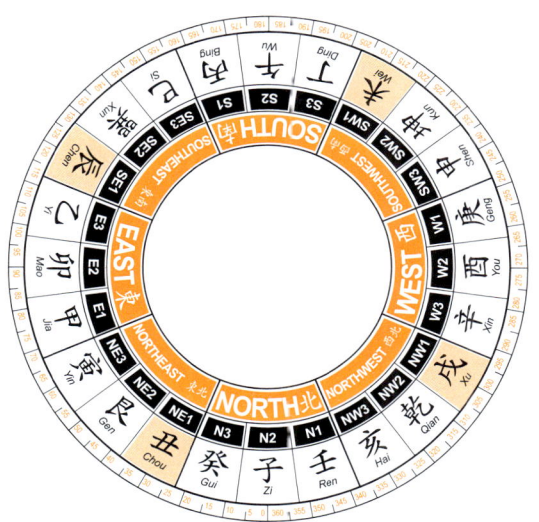

Ideally, you should not have a bathroom or toilet located in these areas of your home above and Sha Qi external features such as pylons, T-junctions, Dead Tree should be avoided. The Sha Qi in the Personal Grand Duke Sector is extremely strong and so all efforts to avoid spending a lot of time in it should be made. It goes without saying that the Personal Grand Duke Sector of your home is not the ideal spot for a bedroom! The Sha Qi in this area of the home is so strong in fact that it is difficult for any further negative Qi to enter!

Personal Clash Directions

Your home will contain Personal Clash Sectors. Spending time in these areas of your home will bring up problems in your life with significant others. As a Star 1 person, you will find your Personal Clash Sectors in the following directions:

Personal Clash Directions for Male

MALE Birth Year	Personal Clash Sector	Direction
1913, 1949, 1985, 2021	未 Wei Goat	西南1 Southwest 1
1922, 1958, 1994, 2030	辰 Chen Dragon	東南1 Southeast 1
1931, 1967, 2003, 2039	丑 Chou Ox	東北1 Northeast 1
1940, 1976, 2012, 2048	戌 Xu Dog	西北1 Northwest 1

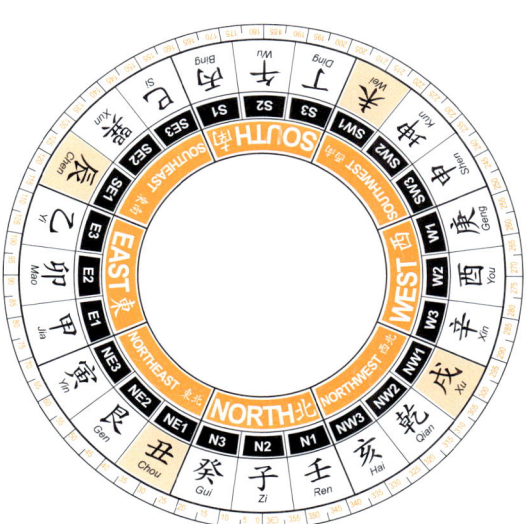

Personal Clash Directions for Female

FEMALE Birth Year	Personal Grand Duke	Direction
1919, 1955, 1991, 2027	丑 *Chou* **Ox**	東北 1 **Northeast 1**
1928, 1964, 2000, 2036	戌 *Xu* **Dog**	西北 1 **Northwest 1**
1937, 1973, 2009, 2045	未 *Wei* **Goat**	西南 1 **Southwest 1**
1946, 1982, 2018, 2054	辰 *Chen* **Dragon**	東南 1 **Southeast 1**

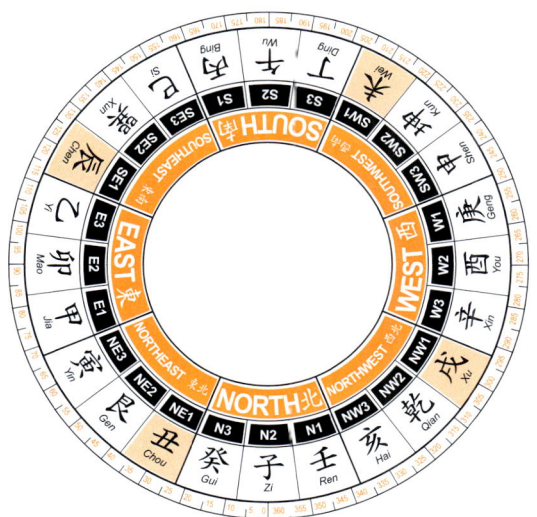

The locations above are a bad place for important features of your home such as the main door, bedroom and kitchen. You should seek to avoid these sectors in the same way you avoid your Personal Grand Duke Sector.

Flying Stars Effects

Each year, the Xuan Kong Flying Stars fly into a different section of a property, be it your residence or your work space. The effects that these Nine Stars have on you will be different depending on your Life Star. In this section you can find out how different Flying Stars in different sectors will effect you with regards to Feng Shui.

The Flying Stars have both negative and positive attributes, but which facets will show when you see a particular Star, depends on the timeliness and the period.

A few of the Nine Stars are inherently negative, a few are inherently positive in nature and some can be both good and bad. Even then, we must remember that the Stars have the capacity to manifest either their positive or negative facets because in Feng Shui, nothing is ever inherently bad or good forever.

When it comes to Flying Stars, it is important to remember this key principle: Forms activate the Stars and the Stars in turn influence the People. This is what you should keep in mind as you read about the effects of the Nine Stars on your Life Star.

1 ★ → 6 White Life

The effects of the visiting #1 White Star on a 6 White Life:

In terms of Feng Shui effects, the presence of the #1 White is likely to bring about positive developments for the reputation and stature of Star 6 people. You will find it a useful Star for you if you want a boost in your image or authority at the workplace. In general, it is good if you hold a powerful position or are in senior management at the workplace. Furthermore, the #1 White is also good for financial intelligence, and it will be particularly useful for you if you work in the investment sector or deal with money on a regular basis. Star 6 politicians or those of this Star who dabble in the political arena will also derive benefits.

2 ★ → 6 White Life

The effects of the visiting #2 Black Star on a 6 White Life:

In terms of Feng Shui effects, the presence of the #2 Black brings about health problems for the Star 6 person. In particular, you can expect gastrointestinal issues. Women and pregnant women need to exercise caution as the #2 Black also brings problems for your reproductive system. The presence of the Star can have adverse effects for your mental and emotional well being, inducing paranoia or insecurity. In some cases, it might even bring about hallucinations, but this is only in extreme cases, if your physical health is already weak.

3★ → 6 White Life

The effects of the visiting #3 Jade Star on a 6 White Life:

In terms of Feng Shui effects, the presence of the #3 Jade brings about problems associated with the physical body, increasing the chance of accidental injury. Be careful during high risk activities such as sports or driving. There will also be the risk of injury through the use of sharp metal implements or tools. Beyond that, ill health can also plague Star 6 folk affected by the energies of the #3 Jade. This will come in the form of headaches and migraines for the most part, and other general, stress-induced illnesses may arise.

4 ★ → 6 White Life

The effects of the visiting #4 Green Star on a 6 White Life:

In terms of Feng Shui effects, the presence of the #4 Green bodes ill for relationships, particularly romantic ones. In some extreme cases, when external features are negative, the #4 Green can bring about the end of relationships. If this isn't the case then you can expect your relationships to burdened and negatively impacted to some lesser degree. Star 6 women will bear the brunt of the #4 Green in terms of physical health. If you're a woman, take extra care, as you might be ill more frequently than usual. In general, this Star can also cast a pall on your mental well being and create moments of depression and melancholy.

5★ → 6 White Life

The effects of the visiting #5 Yellow Star on a 6 White Life:

In terms of Feng Shui effects, the presence of the #5 Yellow brings about some significant health concerns for most people living in the sector. In some extreme cases, where the external Feng Shui is also negative, then there is the likelihood of serious conditions such as cancer. Star 6 men may find that they struggle with career issues with the presence of the #5 Yellow. You will find it hard to make inroads and move up the career ladder, and in some negative cases you actually move backwards in your career or encounter insurmountable problems.

6 ★ → 6 White Life

The effects of the visiting **#6 White Star** on a **6 White Life:**

In terms of Feng Shui effects, the presence of the #6 White is good for wealth luck. It brings about an increased likelihood of secondary income opportunities. In your main line of work, it could also bring about a raise or some other financial benefits if you're a full-time salaried employee. But if there are negative external features present, then the #6 White brings about health problems and complications, particularly those involving the lungs. Its energy also encourages fights and arguments between family members living together under one roof.

7★ → 6 White Life

The effects of the visiting **#7 Red Star** on a **6 White Life:**

In terms of Feng Shui effects, the presence of the #7 Red brings about a strong Metal presence as this Star is also of the Metal element. As such, this combination brings about the Sword-Fighting Sha because it denotes two Metals clashing with each other. What this means is that there is bound to be unrest and conflict among people living in this area. This is particularly true for brothers living in the same house or sector. In general, the #7 Red brings unhealthy rivalry and competition to all your relationships, leading to feelings of discontent and possible resentment. Finally, this Star also denotes the risk of theft and robbery.

8★ → 6 White Life

The effects of the visiting #8 White Star on a 6 White Life:

In terms of Feng Shui effects, the presence of the #8 White is a good one for Star 6 people involved in careers related to property investment or real estate. It is a Star that is also likely to bring about auspicious wealth luck and good boost in your reputation and stature. However, if there are negative features outside this sector, then the presence of the #8 White leads to mental and emotional unrest and turbulence.

9★ → 6 White Life

The effects of the visiting #9 Purple Star on a 6 White Life:

In terms of Feng Shui effects, the presence of the #9 Purple is not very auspicious, and is also known in classical Chinese Feng Shui terms as 'Fire Burning the Heaven's Gate.' Star 6 children will be affected by this Star in terms of temperament – they will be rebellious and misbehave more than usual. This is particularly true for male Star 6 children. Furthermore, this Star also brings physical illness or complications involving blood pressure, and in some more serious cases, the brain.

五行

THE FIVE ELEMENTS

This is a cycle where the elements "produce" one another in terms of providing or helping the growth of another. In the case of Water, then, it produces nourishment for trees and plants (i.e. Wood). An element that produces another element means that it strengthens and grows the element that it produces. Here are some simple metaphors might help you visualize this better:

Water waters soil, producing Wood
Wood makes kindling, producing Fire
Fire makes ashes, producing Earth
Earth is mined, producing Metal
Metal melts, producing Water

Controlling Cycle

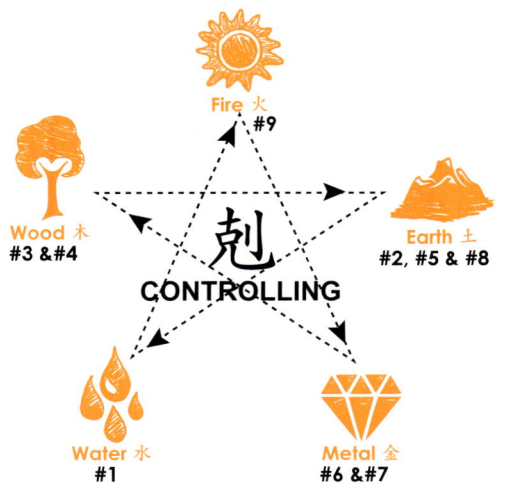

In this cycle,

| Fire controls Metal |
| Metal controls Wood |
| Wood controls Earth |
| Earth controls Water |
| Water controls Fire |

This is a cycle where the elements keep each under in "control": an element is countered or subjugated by its controlling element. In this instance, for example, the element of Water controls Fire by putting it out. Here are some simple metaphors to help you visualize it better:

Water extinguishes Fire
Fire melts Metal
Metal cuts Wood
Wood roots tightly grip Earth
Earth contains Water

Weakening Cycle

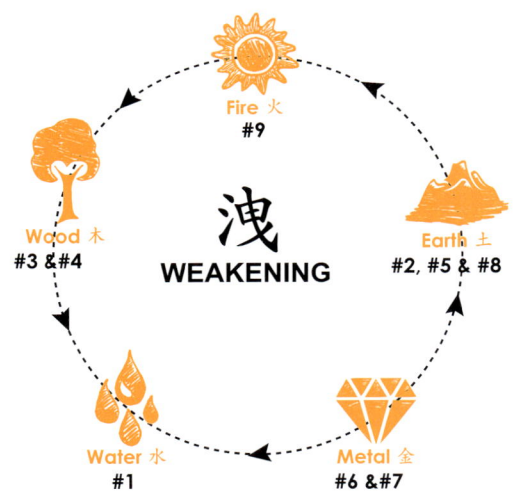

In this cycle,

| Water weakens Metal |
| Metal weakens Earth |
| Earth weakens Fire |
| Fire weakens Wood |
| Wood weakens Water |

The Weakening Cycle can be best understood as the reverse of the Productive Cycle, in that the strength of the element is weakened by another in order to keep it in check. Remember, the key to Qi in Feng Shui is balance, and different elements keep other elements from becoming too strong. For example, Wood absorbs Water and therefore weakens it. Again, here are some metaphors for easier visualization:

Water can be partly absorbed by Wood
Wood can be partly burnt by Fire
Fire can be diminished with Earth
Earth is weakened when mined for Metal
Metal is corroded by Water

The following table shows you the Annual Stars for the year 2000 to 2026.

Examine it and figure out where your room lies; in which sector. Take note of the element of that sector and remember that as a Star 6 person, your element is Metal.

2002, 2011, 2020

巽 SE Xun	離 S Li	坤 SW Kun
6 White METAL	2 Black EARTH	4 Green WOOD
5 Yellow EARTH	7 Red METAL	9 Purple FIRE
1 White WATER	3 Jade WOOD	8 White EARTH
艮 NE Gen	坎 N Kan	乾 NW Qian

(震 Zhen on left / 兌 W Dui on right)

2003, 2012, 2021

巽 SE Xun	離 S Li	坤 SW Kun
5 Yellow EARTH	1 White WATER	3 Jade WOOD
4 Green WOOD	6 White METAL	8 White EARTH
9 Purple FIRE	2 Black EARTH	7 Red METAL
艮 NE Gen	坎 N Kan	乾 NW Qian

2004, 2013, 2022

巽 SE Xun	離 S Li	坤 SW Kun
4 Green WOOD	9 Purple FIRE	2 Black EARTH
3 Jade WOOD	5 Yellow EARTH	7 Red METAL
8 White EARTH	1 White WATER	6 White METAL
艮 NE Gen	坎 N Kan	乾 NW Qian

2005, 2014, 2023

巽 SE Xun	離 S Li	坤 SW Kun
3 Jade WOOD	8 White EARTH	1 White WATER
2 Black EARTH	4 Green WOOD	6 White METAL
7 Red METAL	9 Purple FIRE	5 Yellow EARTH
艮 NE Gen	坎 N Kan	乾 NW Qian

2006, 2015, 2024

巽 SE Xun	離 S Li	坤 SW Kun
2 Black EARTH	7 Red METAL	9 Purple FIRE
1 White WATER	3 Jade WOOD	5 Yellow EARTH
6 White METAL	8 White EARTH	4 Green WOOD
艮 NE Gen	坎 N Kan	乾 NW Qian

2007, 2016, 2025

巽 SE Xun	離 S Li	坤 SW Kun
1 White WATER	6 White METAL	8 White EARTH
9 Purple FIRE	2 Black EARTH	4 Green WOOD
5 Yellow EARTH	7 Red METAL	3 Jade WOOD
艮 NE Gen	坎 N Kan	乾 NW Qian

2008, 2017, 2026

巽 SE Xun	離 S Li	坤 SW Kun
9 Purple FIRE	5 Yellow EARTH	7 Red METAL
8 White EARTH	1 White WATER	3 Jade WOOD
4 Green WOOD	6 White METAL	2 Black EARTH
艮 NE Gen	坎 N Kan	乾 NW Qian

2000, 2009, 2018

巽 SE Xun	離 S Li	坤 SW Kun
8 White EARTH	4 Green WOOD	6 White METAL
7 Red METAL	9 Purple FIRE	2 Black EARTH
3 Jade WOOD	5 Yellow EARTH	1 White WATER
艮 NE Gen	坎 N Kan	乾 NW Qian

2001, 2010, 2019

巽 SE Xun	離 S Li	坤 SW Kun
7 Red METAL	3 Jade WOOD	5 Yellow EARTH
6 White METAL	8 White EARTH	1 White WATER
2 Black EARTH	4 Green WOOD	9 Purple FIRE
艮 NE Gen	坎 N Kan	乾 NW Qian

These Annual Stars shows you the location of the Stars in a property for the duration of the years specified. Based on the year, the Annual Stars will be located in different sectors of the house. Accordingly, different Annual Stars will affect the Feng Shui of your room in different years.

If the Annual Star of your bedroom is of the same element as your Life Star then the outcome is likely to be prosperous (Productive Cycle). If the Annual Star is your Life Star's controlling element (Controlling Cycle), then the result is likely to be stressful – although this combination is still desirable. But if the Annual Star element is the countering element (Countering Cycle) of your Life Star, then the combination is an unfavorable or inauspicious one for you. (Special note: the #5 Yellow Star is generally an undesirable Annual Star for your bedroom regardless of your Life Star.)

Think about the way the element of the Annual Star and your element (Metal) interact.

Besides the Annual Stars of the year, there also other factors to be considered. These include the Flying Stars chart of your specific house or property with the Sitting and Facing Stars. Advanced students may want to read *Xuan Kong Flying Stars Feng Shui* for further information. These Stars also affect the evaluation of the impact of the Xuan Kong Flying Stars on your property. There are many other ways of assessing the Feng Shui of a property, and it's important to understand that all these factors play an important and related role.

Characteristics of Star 6

We all have our "good days" and "bad days". Feng Shui seeks to help isolate why this happens and provide advice that you can use to make every day a "good day" where you are in your element. This section outlines the good and bad characteristics of your Life Star. In a positive sector of your house or work, the positive attributes of your Life Star will be further enhanced, and you will display more of these characteristics. In a negative sector, the positive attributes will be diminished and the negative attributes will begin to show through. Your bad characteristics will take center stage.

The Good

Prestige

Star 6 individuals benefit from an aura of respectability, stature, and authority. This combination means that you create a very impressive influence. At your best, you tend to be the leader who sets the pace for others, but this trait and your gravitas has more to do with your upstanding commitment to justice and fairness than your charm or likeability.

Straightforward

The Life Star 6 personality is straight-talking and straight-shooting. There are no curves to your approach, simply because once you believe in something to be right you set your mind to it and rarely waver from your approach or perspective. As such, you are often honest in your speech, and don't place a high premium on having to sweeten your words to make them palatable for others. Because of this, you are not the kind of person who will flatter others or ingratiate yourself in order to curry favour or earn a good impression.

Just

Out of all the Life Stars, the Star 6 person places the most priority on justice and fairness. You dislike seeing injustice being committed in this world, and your instinct is always to fight for those who suffer from it. You uphold laws and rules and adhere to a code of ethics and high morals standards. You and are not easily swayed from your point of view. You tend to adopt a realistic perspective and your are strong in your observations and judgments.

Loyal

Part of the Life Star 6 character make-up is an investment in loyalty and honor. In that respect, you tend to be committed to the relationships you forge and are in it for the long-haul. You tend to see a relationship as something to be adhered to and dislike flimsy, wishy-washy, tenuous connections with other people.

壞

The Bad

Proud

At an unhealthy level, your sense of prestige can quickly sour and become something akin to pride. You are competitive by nature and everything is a competition to you. When you are in a negative frame of mind you can become hung up on the prospect of losing. It becomes important for you to keep up appearances at any cost; after all your reputation and stature are the result of a lot of hard work. The idea of losing face is so frightening to you that you can make the wrong decisions in an effort to preserve it.

Stubborn

While you're adherence to rules and ideals can be admirable, at other times it can become your weakness. This is when you start to lack imagination and become averse to doing things another way, even when that way yield better results. You can cross over the line and simply become hard-headed and stubborn. Being stubborn makes you unable to change your tactics or your approach even when it would benefit you and you can easily for you to struggle down the wrong path when you should know better.

Distant

You have the tendency to be emotionally-removed and distant from others because you set up barriers around yourself. While living a principled life can sometimes be lonely, it does not have to be as lonely as you make it. One of the weaknesses of Star 6 people is that they set themselves up as above and beyond reproach, and hence above and beyond others. This means that you tend to have problems emotionally relating to people close to you, and may sometimes lack the ability to accept others as they are.

Insecure

When out of balance, the Star 6 character also falls prey to feelings of insecurity. This is when you typically focus inward and become self-indulgent to the point where you start to lose perspective. You may easily become melancholic and depressed, entering into a vicious cycle and refusing to spur yourself on to action once more. As such, you become insecure over your own accomplishments and abilities.

職業和財富

CAREER AND WEALTH

Characteristics at Work

As a Star 6 person, you may display some of these basic characteristics in professional situations at the workplace and in relation to your career. Being aware of your own key characteristics will help you understand why you act and react to situations, people, and tasks in the way you do.

This section outlines the good and bad characteristics of your Life Star. In a positive sector of your house or work, the positive attributes of your Life Star will be further enhanced, and you will display more of these characteristics. In a negative sector, the positive attributes will be diminished and the negative attributes will begin to show through. Your bad characteristics will take center stage.

• Practical

You have a realistic view of things and while on the job you are someone who is task-oriented and practical. This means that you efficiently employ your judgment and skills to get things done quickly and properly when you're at your best. When you become aware of a situation or problem you don't just accurately recognize what needs to be done – you do it, too.

• Action-oriented

It follows, then, that the Star 6 personality at work is an action-orientated one. You have come to recognize that the only way to meet targets, achieve goals or complete tasks is to take action instead of day dreaming. You are impressively efficient and your superiors and colleagues recognize this and rely on you more so that anyone else at the workplace.

• Perfectionist

Just as you are a stickler for rules, you tend to be a stickler for details. This works in your favor in your job and in your career, as it's one of your characteristics that ensures you always turn in an excellent piece of work or enables you to leave no idea

unturned. You live out your day to day life abiding by your own principles and you adhere to them with the same diligence.

• Independent

You tend to like things done in a certain way, and as such your best moments on the job tend to be when you can get things done on your own. You're someone who feels like others slow you down or that others are a liability. You believe that if you want something done right you have to do it yourself, so you do.

Suitable Job Roles

- ## Engineer, accountant

You're also suited to working alone and on technically challenging work which absorbs your interest. The fields of engineering demand the discipline and mathematical, inflexible approach you favor. You have strong self esteem and rarely need to be in a 'team' in order to feel appreciated or valued. Your practical mind, keen observation skills and sound judgment render you ideal for independent work in engineering or accounting.

• Civil servant

Because of your strict adherence to the rules and laws and established order of things, you are likely to find that working in the civil service plays up to your strengths. You tend to enjoy the strict organizational structure because it rarely asks you to break the rules or step out of your comfort zone and this is something you value in your job.

• Politician

Whilst it is true that you may not have the charm or flashy PR skills necessary for unpolitical situations, you're probably one of the best candidates for a life in politics due to your steadfast commitment to justice, and the rule of law. As a leader, you use your stature,

power, and authority for the common good. You seek to help others instead of using your standing to further your own selfish goals.

• Lawyer, legal work

Legal work plays perfectly to your strengths and desires. You will also find playing an important role in upholding the law will be extremely rewarding. Your due diligence and meticulousness is also utilized well in this role, as a lot of legal work consists of pain staking poring-through of documents, clauses, and statutes. You leave no stone unturned and you always look for the morally correct solution which are two traits that will go down well in the detail-oriented field of legal work.

Career and Wealth Guide

• Be humble

Pride comes before a fall, they say, and that is something worth thinking about. Most importantly, you must be able to distinguish between confidence from pride, because otherwise you are naturally inclined to see everyone else as somehow lesser than you, or unworthy of your attention. Throughout your career, however, you will meet people from all levels of life – most who do not share your principles and beliefs – who will prove to helpful and your potential allies. Don't miss out on the benefits they bring because you feel superior.

• Network

Being social is not something that comes easily to you, and you work best alone. This is fine and well if you are in a job that is largely solitary, but the reality of work life in the modern age is that a strong social network is necessary if you wish to get ahead. Learn how to forge useful connections to people who can help you further your career and teach you things to advance and improve your knowledge – this will prove invaluable.

• Accept failure as inevitable

Everyone must fail in life occasionally. In fact, it's a truism that out of the ashes of failure, new opportunities can be be born, because you're forced to reevaluate your strategy and think of something different. If you don't learn this lesson then your career will suffer as otherwise - being proud, and very scrupulous - you may be inclined to shy away from potentially lucrative scenarios if you see a risk of failure. Do not be afraid of failure. A failure is not the end; when one door closes another one always opens.

- **More adventurous at work, more cautious with money**

You can be very conservative in your decision making and, at times, you will miss out on things that you could have had if only you were able to be more forward-thinking and inventive. Where money matters are concerned, however, you can sometimes be careless or lose your focus and interest, thereby sustaining losses. Be more cautious with the documents you sign or the investment ventures you get into.

• Share your authority

Sometimes being the leader or the responsible one can take a heavy toll on your work quality and sense of enthusiasm or passion. It will be good for you to learn to delegate not just the menial work but the important responsibilities, too, because this will also help you forge important connections that can help you weather good times and bad.

Famous Personalities :

Carlos Slim Helu,
Charles F Feeney,
Mark Cuban,
Stephenie Meyer

人際關係

RELATIONSHIPS

Guide for Relationships

As a Star 6 person, you need some help when it comes to matters of the heart. This is not because you're an unfeeling person, but simply because you're not used to expressing feelings in overt ways – it makes you feel uncomfortable. Despite this, you have a natural charm that draws people to you, and your attractiveness can, in large part, be attributed to your aura of power and prestige. Once you do manage to grab someone's attention, you will need a little help to guide you along the way in maintaining it.

You tend to have realistic expectations of everything that you approach in life, and this includes your love life. You have a strong view on how things should be a done and a very sturdy sense of self, and because of this you expect to have a lot of freedom and to be granted it. It is not so much that you want the freedom to play around – in fact, the opposite is true. However, you need the space to do what you want and to conduct your life on your own terms, which is a fairly healthy character trait unless you end up isolating yourself and blocking out those who care.

While your thinking seems conservative, and indeed you err on the side of caution in most things, in matters of love your thoughts can become easily ruled by emotions. Because you're not accustomed to with your innermost feelings, this can manifest in unpredictable or even moody behavior, which can occasionally leave your partner befuddled and confused.

In marriage, you tend to be very devoted and loyal, so in the long run you do make a good partner – but in order for this to be possible you need to be more willing to share your feelings and overcome your emotional distance. Star 6 men tend to adopt the position of power and authority in the marriage itself, somehow falling into the traditional role of material 'provider' while neglecting their wife's emotions and feelings. This is not done out of spite so much as cluelessness – so if you work on this aspect, you will find that your domestic life will much more harmonious.

Star 6 in relationships:

Although Star 6 people may appear disinterested in romance, they are strongly possessive of their partners. They often need to cultivate a stronger emotional or romantic nature.

健康

HEALTH

Guide for Health

Body parts and organs that are related to Star 6: Lungs, large intestine, liver, heart.

Your Star 6 represents the lungs, liver and heart, and the large intestine. When you are struck down with health problems, these are the organs and systems which are likely to be affected.

The ailments which you need to watch out for include respiratory disease, lung disease, bronchitis, and anything involving your breathing and your nose, such as sinus allergies. You will also need to watch out for brain and cerebellum related complications. Furthermore, you are at risk of eye problem, inflammation of the kidneys and illnesses which strike in the stomach and bowels. Recurring constipation and hemorrhoids are a risk for Star 6 people. Skin problems and allergies will also be a common problem. The good news is that as a rule, Star 6 people are generally hardy and very sturdy in health, but when you do fall ill, you fall hard and whatever is plaguing you tends to attack with a vengeance.

You need to come to pay as much as attention to your physical health as you do to other aspects of your life. Consider the more practical angles of health care as you become older in terms of a health care plan or insurance. Furthermore, you tend to be reckless once in awhile with your diet and have the penchant to over-indulge in alcohol or other substances when you want to simply 'let loose' and have fun, but this should be done in moderation so as not to tax your liver and heart.

Potential health concerns:

Headaches & migraine

Blemishes, boils, pimples, acne & cysts appearing on the face

Brain & head-related ailments

Coughs & parched throat

COMPATIBILITY WITH OTHER LIFE STARS

This section examines your compatibility as a Star 6 person with other people who have the same and different Stars. No person goes through life completely alone. Relationships with others form the bedrock of good career networking. Friendships and relations with loved ones, spouses, partners and family make everything worth while. It is necessary to understand how compatible people with different Stars are to prevent conflict and missed opportunities. Bear in mind that issues of compatibility are not definite or set in stone. There are exceptions to every rule. In addition, **the quality of Feng Shui** in your environment helps dictate whether positive or negative traits in people manifest themselves and thus it weighs in on the quality of your relationships with those people. This section serves as a good guide on your relationships with other people of different Stars.

At a glance, Star 6 people are generally quite compatible with fellow Star 6 people, as you will both encourage and complement each other. But it will be necessary for both parties to identify the strengths and weaknesses and decide on what role each play before proceeding with a partnership, as both of you are excellent leaders but lack practical talents, patience and initiative.

Star 6 people will also have good relationships with Star 7 people. Both parties can benefit when you come together and natural cooperation makes long term partnerships possible. You will also do well with Stars 2, 5, and 8, because these are Earth Stars and Earth produces Metal. Hence, in business, work, and wealth, people of these Stars are likely to become your allies and help you overcome problems and promote your status. Similarly, your interactions with people of Stars 3 and 4 are likely to produce good outcomes, particularly within professional relationships.

You are likely to run into problems with Star 9 people, since it Star 9 is a Fire Star and Fire counters or weakens Metal. This could be bad for you especially in terms of wealth, and where personalities are concerned, friction is likely to arise if you become too close with a Star 9 person. Your relationship with a Star 1 person may be seem to work on the surface, but no long term understanding can be reached and no deeper connection can be made since Star 1 is a Water Star and Metal produces Water, and Water in the long run will weaken Metal.

The chart below lists element people or sectors you can utilize to improve your compatibility with other Star people.

Star 6	Compatibility with others Stars (Individuals)	Seek help from this element people or use this sector
	Stars 2, 5 & 8 (Earth Element)	Metal
	Stars 3 & 4 (Wood Element)	Water
	Stars 6 & 7 (Metal Element)	Fire
	Star 9 (Fire Element)	Earth
	Star 1 (Water Element)	Wood

巽 SE Xun	離 S Li	坤 SW Kun
4 Green WOOD	**9** Purple FIRE	**2** Black EARTH
3 Jade WOOD (震 E Zhen)	**5** Yellow EARTH	**7** Red METAL (兌 W Dui)
8 White EARTH	**1** White WATER	**6** White METAL
艮 NE Gen	坎 N Kan	乾 NW Qian

The following pages will explain in detail the compatibility factor of a Star 6 person with people of all other nine Stars through the Compatibility Meter. The Compatibility Guides give you tips for managing the relationships in question.

| **6** White | compatibility with | **1** White |

Compatibility Meter

When you and Star 1 person get together, the match is likely to be lukewarm and only productive in the short-term. This is largely due to the fact that the Water element in Star 1 weakens the Metal element in Star 6 in the long run. At the start, the match will seem fairly complimentary, and if it's a friendship, it will even appear as though both of you like each other. This is an illusion created by the tendency for Star 1 people to employ diplomacy in an effort to get along with everyone they meet. They may be friendly and agreeable at first simply because they do not seek out conflict with others. Although they can be good workers who can be productive without excessive intervention, their work style may not sit well with you. They can chop and change and become bored easily and they may not stick to plans

that you create. In addition, they can be just as stubborn as you. In the long term, these differing work styles can mean that you wish to go your separate ways in matters of business. Star 1 people have more to offer you as friends or even romantic partners.

Compatibility Guide

A friendly or romantic connection can be made to work if you apply focus in solving personal differences. Help them to understand that you find clarity of expression important. You may find that their listening skills allow you to open up which will be good for you. You will also need to learn to be a little more unpredictable if you wish to hold their attention, otherwise they may be tempted to leave. They do not share your unwavering sense of loyalty so marriage may not be on the cards for a Star 1 and a Star 6. Finally, Star 1 individuals also like to call the shots at least some of the time so some give and take will be in order to give things a better chance of working.

| **6** White | compatibility with | **2** Black |

Compatibility Meter

When you and a Star 2 person get together, the result is likely to be very beneficial for both of you. Star 2 individuals can be thought of as weak minded to an extent and they will be immediately impressed by your powerful presence. Indeed, you can teach them a lot about how to make a stand on important issues because when left to their own devices they are submissive. You work best in situations where you can lead and delegate and Star 2 people work best when given a task to do, although you may need to help motivate them from time to time. They are diligent and practical, like you, and resourceful which means they can get things done with a little encouragement. In a friendship or a romantic relationship, you will enjoy a close connection. You may come to view each

other as soul mates as you are both sincere and honest of heart, with the need to know and learn everything about the other person in order to support and nurture them. In the long run, this is likely to be a mutually-beneficial connection. Your trust and loyalty in them will not be misplaced and as a person of principle you will appreciate this. As time passes they may help you learn to show your loving and caring side.

Compatibility Guide

While your relationship is very auspicious, there will be points of friction that can cause some significant problems. Because you're someone who is unable to deal very well with emotions, you must try to exercise more patience if this person disappoints you. Star 2 people will respond well to you if you strive to understand and appreciate their efforts instead of running them down. Be less stubborn and demanding and reap the rewards.

| **6** White | compatibility with | **3** Jade |

Compatibility Meter

When you and a Star 3 person come together, the result is likely to be complicated.

Although you and a Star 3 person start off on the right foot, friction can quickly develop. A Star 3 individual live by his or her own principles and rules by you, but these principles and rules may not necessarily align with yours. When this does happen, conflict will be brought out into the open because you are both frank and straight talking. Disagreements will always be discussed in a reasonable and open way but if essential characteristics are at odds then friction will continue to develop over time. Romantically, if a Star 3 person falls for you, you may find their pursuit off putting. When they fall in love they fall hard and this does not sit well with your reserved, controlled approach to romance.

With that said, when a Star 3 person finds their muse they will be loyal and this trait in a partner is of paramount importance to you.

Compatibility Guide

Both you and the Star 3 person will have the tendency to be stubborn, and where you're concerned in particular you don't like to 'lose' and give up easily. This can only make the relationship a tense and fraught one that is punctuated by regular fights and arguments if you allow it to. To make this work, you will have to be the first on to give up your pride – and if you can, your relationship can be civil. If you do become involved romantically you must make a concerted effort to express yourselves and be more loving if things are to work.

| **6** White | compatibility with | **4** White |

Compatibility Meter

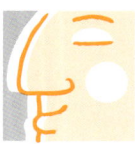

When you and a Star 4 person come together, there is likely to be conviviality with a hint of reserve. The typical Star 4 person is soft and subtle, keeping others at a certain distance for fear of getting hurt. You keep others at a distance because you do not know how to express feelings! The result is that your interactions can be cold although this is not because of any ill feeling. At work, they are best suited to tasks which involve creativity. You may find that they bring flexibility to the table and come up with options you had not considered. Romantically, they have different expectations from you. They like to cultivate dramatic, exciting relationships whilst you look for stable, loyal companionship. However, with all of this said, because there is strong basic affinity and mutual attraction

between Star 6 and Star 4 people, conflict and arguments are likely to be short lived and easily put in the past.

Compatibility Guide

You may have to work hard to make a business relationship work and to make up for the deficiencies in practicality you believe Star 4 people possess. You must come to accept that they do not always respond well to your direct approach and may simply withdraw into themselves the harder you push. They also do not share your iron commitment to certain rules and ideals which means that they may live their lives differently. In terms of a romantic relationship, if you cannot meet each other halfway in terms of understanding, then it's best to cut your losses and simply focus on a friendship.

| 6 White | compatibility with | 5 Yellow |

Compatibility Meter

Regardless of whether the connection between you and a Star 5 person is personal or professional, the outcome is likely to be good as your relationship with a Star 2 person. Mutual respect and a sense of shared camaraderie will develop as you both see qualities you are proud of in yourselves in one another. Star 5 individuals, like you, are independent and make natural leaders. You are opinionated and stubborn and Star 2 people can be headstrong. This can lead to some conflict but it is likely to be short lived because of their ability to take an impartial look at problems and come up with solutions. They do possess a sensitive side but it is unlikely that you will gain access to it because you lack the expressive tendencies needed to coax them into revealing it. This means that any feelings between you will

remain unspoken. Despite their strong and commanding behavior their shyness presents a barrier that you must overcome. Fortunately, you are anything but meek and with time this can be done.

Compatibility Guide

What will help this connection along is complete honesty, because if either you or the Star 5 person senses that the other is being hypocritical or less than honest, the relationship is likely to end very quickly. This connection works well as a strong friendship, and what will keep both your interest piqued is the mutual commitment to learning and expanding your knowledge together. Power struggles may plague business relationships as you are both independent and autonomous, unsuited to following orders from others.

| 6 White | compatibility with | 6 White |

Compatibility Meter

When you and Star 6 person get together, the effect is likely to be beneficial and a long lasting connection may well result. You will find that you respect them because they, like you, are committed to their principles. This validates your world view and makes you feel less alone in the way you live your life. You have similar personalities, and thus can understand each other even when the other is unable to convey his or her emotions. As such, the relationship will work well in terms of a friendship or a relationship, as you will both encourage each other to strive for your potential instead of excluding or denigrating the other. When you come to work together, you may have some trouble in that you are both more suited to delegating than actually doing work. You will need a clear idea of who is to do what if you are to succeed.

Compatibility Guide

Although you and another Star 6 person are likely to enjoy an excellent relationship, there are instances where you may not be able to get along, and the effort to keep it going is too much. If this is a romance and you think things are going off the rails, iit will be best to end it early while you're still in each others good graces and in harmony, as then there is likelihood that you'll still remain friends. If you're in a business partnership, make sure to end all financial and career connections to each other and there will also be the possibility that you can still get together every so often as friends.

| **6** White | compatibility with | **7** Red |

Compatibility Meter

When Star 6 people get together with Star 7 people, the results are complex. It is fair to say that Star 7 individuals are extremely outgoing, exciting and bubbly. Their taste lies in extravagance and fun. They can either share this with you or you can find it hard to empathize with their choices and priorities. Your entire life revolves around a higher set of ideals whilst theirs revolves around what you see as cheap self indulgent thrills! You may find their arrogance and selfishness jarring and hard to deal with but their differences are their great strength. if you can learn to harness them in a professional capacity then you may be able to make use of their social graces. They, being great with other people, are adept at networking and closing deals. These are skills you may have use for. If

this is a romance or a friendship, there is unlikely to be any sparkling chemistry, despite the best efforts of the Star 7 individual to liven things up. You simply do not have much in common on a personal level.

Compatibility Guide

Before you proceed with your relationship with the Star 7 person, it will be important to feel things out to ensure that you're both on the same page. Otherwise, in the long run, you're bound to bore each other. Furthermore, do not be blunt and straightforward in pointing out the flaws in the Star 7 person – you need to be diplomatic and soften your words, in order to keep them talking to you and trusting you. The most important person in the life of a Star 7 person is themselves and bursting their bubble will not yield any benefit for you.

| **6** White | compatibility with | **8** White |

Compatibility Meter

When Star 6 people get together with Star 8 people, the outcome is likely to be favorable for both. Whilst your interactions may not be supercharged with excitement, you are not prone to disagreement. When a Star 8 individual does disagree with you they are unlikely to make a fuss which is ideal and lays the foundations for unhindered co-operation and progress, with you in the driving seat!

This is likely to be an auspicious connection for work and career-related ventures. Both you and the Star 6 person are likely to find common ground in the quest for professional goals and targets, and are likely to help each other along the way. You both do things by the book and there won't be any unwelcome surprises in your interactions. However, your personalities

aren't really geared for total compatibility, so whether or not you get along on a personal level depends on the effort you're willing to make. Even though out and out conflict probably wont arise, difference in opinions are entirely possible

Compatibility Guide

Honesty and straightforwardness works in your favor, here, so don't hesitate to tell the Star 8 person how you really feel. You already tell it straight when it comes to business and friendship and if this is a romantic relationship then you need to do the same when it comes to your feelings. He/she will appreciate the candor, and will return it in kind. If, however, you find that the Star 8 person's response is not encouraging, then keep the relationship cool and distant – particularly if this is a work relationship – and be impartial and matter-of-fact in your communication.

| **6** White | compatibility with | **9** Purple |

Compatibility Meter

When you and a Star 9 person come together, the outcome is likely to be risky.

You will have to proceed with caution in your relationship with the Star 9 person, as there may be initial attraction that can cause you to disregard any well founded misgivings about the long term consequences. You may be drawn in by the Star 9 person, but in the long run the various differences of your personality can be draining. You will find yourself constantly battling with them and their pride means they are unlikely to back down, making your efforts futile.

Compatibility Guide

As this relationship can be problematic in the long run, you need to be on your guard. Be strong and always stand by your principles and don't compromise them for the sake of the Star 9 person. If they cannot appreciate you as you are then a relationship isn't worth pursuing in the first place! If this relationship is meant to last or go somewhere, then it will be important for you both to respect each other and not to vindictively draw attention to each others shortcomings – or this will be the recipe for hurt and resentment.

About Joey Yap

Joey Yap first began learning about Chinese Metaphysics from masters in the field when he was fifteen.

Despite having graduated with a Commerce degree in Accounting, Joey never became an accountant. Instead, he began to give seminars, talks and professional Chinese Metaphysic consultations in Malaysia, Singapore, India, Australia, Canada, England, Germany and the United States, becoming a household name in the field.

By the age of twenty-six, Joey became a self-made millionaire and in 2008, he was listed in The Malaysian Tatler as the Top 300 Most Influential People in Malaysia and Prestige's Top 40 Under 40.

His practical and result-driven take on Feng Shui and BaZi sets him apart from other older, traditional masters and practitioners in the field. He shows people how the ancient teachings can be utilized for tangible REAL world benefits. The success he and his clients enjoy, thanks to his advice, is positive proof that Feng Shui and BaZi Astrology works, whether everyone believes in it or not!

Today, Joey has helped and worked with governments and the wealthiest people in Singapore, Hong Kong, China, Malaysia and Japan. His clients include multinationals, developers, tycoons and royalties. On Bloomberg, he is featured on-air as a regular guest on the subject of Feng Shui annual forecasts. He is retained by twenty-five top Malaysian property developers to help determine suitable candidates to take top management, change their space and Feng Shui mechanism, the way they make decisions, and understand the natural cosmic energies that can influence their decision-making.

Every year he conducts his 'Feng Shui and Astrology' seminar to a crowd of more than 3500 people at the Kuala Lumpur Convention Center. He also takes this annual seminar on a world tour to Frankfurt, San Francisco, New York, Las Vegas, Toronto, Sydney and Singapore.

The Joey Yap Consulting Group is the world's largest and first specialized metaphysics consultation firm. His consultancy, and professional speaking and training engagements with Microsoft, HP, Bloomberg, Citibank, HSBC and many more have seen the benefits of Classical Feng Shui and BaZi find their way into corporate environment and culture. Celebrities, property developers and other large organizations turn to Joey when they need the best.

After years of field-testing and fine-tuning his teachings, he has put together a team in the form of Joey Yap Research International. The objective of this Research Team is to scientifically track and verify the positive impact of Feng Shui and BaZi on subjects and ultimately to assist more people in achieving their life goals.

The Mastery Academy of Chinese Metaphysics which Joey founded teaches thousands of students from all around the world about Classical Feng Shui, Chinese Astrology and Face Reading. Many graduates have gone on to become successful in their own right, becoming sought after consultants, setting up their own consultancy businesses or even becoming educators, passing on Chinese Metaphysics knowledge to others.

Joey has also created the Decision Referential Technology™, offering decision reformation training on how to make better decisions in business and in personal life. He has led his team of highly trained consultants to help clients create more positive change in corporate boardrooms and increase production in their companies, helping people see their business outlook for each year so they may anticipate, plan and execute their strategies successfully.

Joey's work has been featured regularly in various popular global publications and networks like Time, Forbes, the International Herald Tribune and Bloomberg. He has also written columns for The New Straits Times, The Star and The Edge – Malaysia's leading newspapers. He has achieved bestselling author status with over sixty-five books, which have sold more than three million copies to-date.

His success is not limited to matters of Feng Shui and BaZi. Although his success is a product of them, he is also a successful entrepreneur, leading his own companies and property investment portfolio. When not teaching metaphysics or consulting around the world, Joey is a Naruto-fan, avid snowboarder and is crazy for fruits de mer.

Author's personal website :

 www.joeyyap.com

Joey Yap on Facebook:

 www.facebook.com/JoeyYapFB

MASTERY ACADEMY
OF CHINESE METAPHYSICS
Your **Preferred** Choice to the Art & Science of Classical Chinese Metaphysics Studies

Bringing **innovative** techniques
and **creative** teaching methods
to an ancient study.

Mastery Academy of Chinese Metaphysics was established by Joey Yap to play the role of disseminating this Eastern knowledge to the modern world with the belief that this valuable knowledge should be accessible to anyone, anywhere.

Its goal is to enrich people's lives through accurate, professional teaching and practice of Chinese Metaphysics knowledge globally. It is the first academic institution of its kind in the world to adopt the tradition of Western institutions of higher learning - where students are encourage to explore, question and challenge themselves and to respect different fields and branches of study - with the appreciation and respect of classical ideas and applications that have stood the test of time.

The art and science of Chinese Metaphysics studies – be it Feng Shui, BaZi (Astrology), Mian Xiang (Face Reading), ZeRi (Date Selection) or Yi Jing – is no longer a field shrouded with mystery and superstition. In light of new technology, fresher interpretations and innovative methods as well as modern teaching tools like the Internet, interactive learning, e-learning and distance learning, anyone from virtually any corner of the globe, who is keen to master these disciplines can do so with ease and confidence under the guidance and support of the Academy.

It has indeed proven to be a center of educational excellence for thousands of students from over thirty countries across the world; many of whom have moved on to practice classical Chinese Metaphysics professionally in their home countries.

At the Academy, we believe in enriching people's lives by empowering their destinies through the disciplines of Chinese Metaphysics. Learning is not an option - it's a way of life!

MASTERY ACADEMY
OF CHINESE METAPHYSICS™

MALAYSIA
19-3, The Boulevard, Mid Valley City, 59200 Kuala Lumpur, Malaysia
Tel : +603-2284 8080 | Fax : +603-2284 1218
Email   : info@masteryacademy.com
Website : www.masteryacademy.com

Australia, Austria, Canada, China, Croatia, Cyprus, Czech Republic, Denmark, France, Germany, Greece, Hungary, India, Italy, Kazakhstan, Malaysia, Netherlands (Holland), New Zealand, Philippines, Poland, Russian Federation, Singapore, Slovenia, South Africa, Switzerland, Turkey, U.S.A., Ukraine, United Kingdom

www.masteryacademy.com | +603 - 2284 8080

Mastery Academy around the world

www.masteryacademy.com | +603 - 2284 8080

JOEY YAP CONSULTING GROUP

Pioneering Metaphysics - Centric Personal Coaching and Corporate Consulting

The Joey Yap Consulting Group is the world's first specialised metaphysics consultation firm. Founded in 2002 by renown international Feng Shui and BaZi consultant, author and trainer Joey Yap, the Joey Yap Consulting Group is a pioneer in the provision of metaphysics-driven coaching and consultation services for individuals and corporations.

The Group's core consultation practice areas are Feng Shui and BaZi, which are complimented by ancillary services like Date Selection, Face Reading and Yi Jing Divination. The Group's team of highly-trained professional consultants are led by Principal Consultant Joey Yap. The Joey Yap Consulting Group is the firm of choice for corporate captains, entrepreneurs, celebrities and property developers when it comes to Feng Shui and BaZi-related advisory and knowledge.

Across Industries: Our Portfolio of Clients

Our diverse portfolio of both corporate and individual clients from all around the world bears testimony to our experience and capabilities.

Joey Yap Consulting Group is the firm of choice for many of Asia's leading multi-national corporations, listed entities, conglomerates and top-tier property developers when it comes to Feng Shui and corporate BaZi.

Our services also engaged by professionals, prominent business personalities, celebrities, high-profile politicians and people from all walks of life.

JOEY YAP CONSULTING GROUP

Name (Mr./Mrs./Ms.): _____

Contact Details

Tel: _____ Fax: _____

Mobile : _____

E-mail: _____

What Type of Consultation Are You Interested In?
☐ Feng Shui ☐ BaZi ☐ Date Selection ☐ Corporate Events

Please tick if applicable:
☐ Are you a Property Developer looking to engage Joey Yap Consulting Group?

☐ Are you a Property Investor looking for tailor-made packages to suit your investment requirements?

Please attach your name card here.

Thank you for completing this form. Please fax it back to us at:

Malaysia & the rest of the world
Fax : +603-2284 2213   Tel : +603-2284 1213

www.joeyyap.com

Feng Shui Consultations

For Residential Properties
- Initial Land/Property Assessment
- Residential Feng Shui Consultations
- Residential Land Selection
- End-to-End Residential Consultation

For Commercial Properties
- Initial Land/Property Assessment
- Commercial Feng Shui Consultations
- Commercial Land Selection
- End-to-End Commercial Consultation

For Property Developers
- End-to-End Consultation
- Post-Consultation Advisory Services
- Panel Feng Shui Consultant

For Property Investors
- Your Personal Feng Shui Consultant
- Tailor-Made Packages

For Memorial Parks & Burial Sites
- Yin House Feng Shui

BaZi Consultations

Personal Destiny Analysis
- Personal Destiny Analysis for Individuals
- Children's BaZi Analysis
- Family BaZi Analysis

Strategic Analysis for Corporate Organizations
- Corporate BaZi Consultations
- BaZi Analysis for Human Resource Management

Entrepreneurs & Business Owners
- BaZi Analysis for Entrepreneurs

Career Pursuits
- BaZi Career Analysis

Relationships
- Marriage and Compatibility Analysis
- Partnership Analysis

For Everyone
- Annual BaZi Forecast
- Your Personal BaZi Coach

Date Selection Consultations

- **Marriage Date Selection**
- **Caesarean Birth Date Selection**
- **House-Moving Date Selection**
- **Renovation & Groundbreaking Dates**
- **Signing of Contracts**
- **Official Openings**
- **Product Launches**

Corporate Events

Many reputable organizations and instituitions have worked closely with Joey Yap Consulting Group to build a synergistic business relationship by engaging our team of consultants, led by Joey Yap, as speakers at their corporate events.

We tailor our seminars and talks to suit the anticipated or pertinent group of audience. Be it department, subsidiary, your clients or even the entire corporation, we aim to fit your requirements in delivering the intended message(s).

Tel: +603-2284 1213   Email: consultation@joeyyap.com

CHINESE METAPHYSICS REFERENCE SERIES

The Chinese Metaphysics Reference Series is a collection of reference texts, source material, and educational textbooks to be used as supplementary guides by scholars, students, researchers, teachers and practitioners of Chinese Metaphysics.

These comprehensive and structured books provide fast, easy reference to aid in the study and practice of various Chinese Metaphysics subjects including Feng Shui, BaZi, Yi Jing, Zi Wei, Liu Ren, Ze Ri, Ta Yi, Qi Men and Mian Xiang.

The Chinese Metaphysics Compendium

At over 1,000 pages, the *Chinese Metaphysics Compendium* is a unique one-volume reference book that compiles all the formulas relating to Feng Shui, BaZi (Four Pillars of Destiny), Zi Wei (Purple Star Astrology), Yi Jing (I-Ching), Qi Men (Mystical Doorways), Ze Ri (Date Selection), Mian Xiang (Face Reading) and other sources of Chinese Metaphysics.

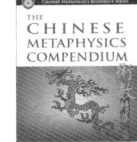

It is presented in the form of easy-to-read tables, diagrams and reference charts, all of which are compiled into one handy book. This first-of-its-kind compendium is presented in both English and the original Chinese, so that none of the meanings and contexts of the technical terminologies are lost.

The only essential and comprehensive reference on Chinese Metaphysics, and an absolute must-have for all students, scholars, and practitioners of Chinese Metaphysics.

The Ten Thousand Year Calendar (Pocket Edition) | The Ten Thousand Year Calendar | Dong Gong Date Selection | The Date Selection Compendium | Plum Blossoms Divination Reference Book | San Yuan Dragon Gate Eight Formations Water Method | Xuan Kong Da Gua Ten Thousand Year Calendar

Bazi Hour Pillar Useful Gods - Wood | Bazi Hour Pillar Useful Gods - Fire | Bazi Hour Pillar Useful Gods - Earth | Bazi Hour Pillar Useful Gods - Metal | Bazi Hour Pillar Useful Gods - Water | Xuan Kong Da Gua Structures Reference Book | Xuan Kong Da Gua 64 Gua Transformation Analysis

    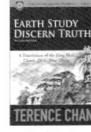

Bazi Structures and Structural Useful Gods - Wood | Bazi Structures and Structural Useful Gods - Fire | Bazi Structures and Structural Useful Gods - Earth | Bazi Structures and Structural Useful Gods - Metal | Bazi Structures and Structural Useful Gods - Water | Xuan Kong Purple White Script | Earth Study Discern Truth Second Edition

www.masteryacademy.com | +603 - 2284 8080

Joey Yap's BaZi Profiling System

Three Levels of BaZi Profiling (English & Chinese versions)

In BaZi Profiling, there are three levels that reflect three different stages of a person's personal nature and character structure.

Level 1 – The Day Master

The Day Master in a nutshell is the BASIC YOU. The inborn personality. It is your essential character. It answers the basic question "WHO AM I". There are ten basic personality profiles – the TEN Day Masters – each with its unique set of personality traits, likes and dislikes.

Level 2 – The Structure

The Structure is your behavior and attitude – in other words, how you use your personality. It expands on the Day Master (Level 1). The structure reveals your natural tendencies in life – are you more controlling, more of a creator, supporter, thinker or connector? Each of the Ten Day Masters express themselves differently through the FIVE Structures. Why do we do the things we do? Why do we like the things we like? – The answers are in our BaZi STRUCTURE.

Level 3 – The Profile

The Profile reveals your unique abilities and skills, the masks that you consciously and unconsciously "put on" as you approach and navigate the world. Your Profile speaks of your ROLES in life. There are TEN roles – or Ten BaZi Profiles. Everyone plays a different role.

What makes you happy and what does success mean to you is different to somebody else. Your sense of achievement and sense of purpose in life is unique to your Profile. Your Profile will reveal your unique style.

The path of least resistance to your success and wealth can only be accessed once you get into your "flow." Your BaZi Profile reveals how you can get FLOW. It will show you your patterns in work, relationship and social settings. Being AWARE of these patterns is your first step to positive Life Transformation.

www.baziprofiling.com

BaZi Collections

Leading Chinese Astrology Master Trainer Joey Yap makes it easy to learn how to unlock your Destiny through your BaZi with these books. BaZi or Four Pillars of Destiny is an ancient Chinese science which enables individuals to understand their personality, hidden talents and abilities as well as their luck cycle, simply by examining the information contained within their birth data.

Understand and appreciate more about this astoundingly accurate ancient Chinese Metaphysical science with this BaZi Collection.

Feng Shui Collection

Must-Haves for Property Analysis!

For homeowners, those looking to build their own home or even investors who are looking to apply Feng Shui to their homes, these series of books provides valuable information from the classical Feng Shui therioes and applications.

In his trademark straight-to-the-point manner, Joey shares with you the Feng Shui do's and dont's when it comes to finding a property with favorable Feng Shui, which is condusive for home living.

Stories & Lessons on Feng Shui Series

All in all, this series is a delightful chronicle of Joey's articles, thoughts and vast experience - as a professional Feng Shui consultant and instructor - that have been purposely refined, edited and expanded upon to make for a light-hearted, interesting yet educational read. And with Feng Shui, BaZi, Mian Xiang and Yi Jing all thrown into this one dish, there's something for everyone.

www.masteryacademy.com | +603 - 2284 8080

Continue Your Journey with Joey Yap Books in Feng Shui

Pure Feng Shui
Pure Feng Shui is Joey Yap's debut with an international publisher, CICO Books, and is a refreshing and elegant look at the intricacies of Classical Feng Shui – now compiled in a useful manner for modern-day readers. This book is a comprehensive introduction to all the important precepts and techniques of Feng Shui practice.

Your Aquarium Here
This book is the first in Fengshuilogy Series, a series of matter-in-fact and useful Feng Shui books designed for the person who wants to do a fuss-free Feng Shui.

Xuan Kong Flying Stars
This book is an essential introductory book to the subject of Xuan Kong Fei Xing, a well-known and popular system of Feng Shui. Learn 'tricks of the trade' and 'trade secrets' to enhance and maximize Qi in your home or office.

Walking the Dragons
Compiled in one book for the first time from Joey Yap's Feng Shui Mastery Excursion Series, the book highlights China's extensive, vibrant history with astute observations on the Feng Shui of important sites and places. Learn the landform formations of Yin Houses (tombs and burial places), as well as mountains, temples, castles, and villages.

The Art of Date Selection: Personal Date Selection
With the *Art of Date Selection: Personal Date Selection*, learn simple, practical methods you can employ to select not just good dates, but personalized good dates. Whether it's a personal activity such as a marriage or professional endeavor such as launching a business, signing a contract or even acquiring assets, this book will show you how to pick the good dates and tailor them to suit the activity in question, as well as avoid the negative ones too!

www.masteryacademy.com | +603 - 2284 8080

Face Reading Collection

Discover Face Reding (English & Chinese versions)

This is a comprehensive book on all areas of Face Reading, covering some of the most important facial features, including the forehead, mouth, ears and even philtrum above your lips. This book eill help you analyse not just your Destiny but help you achieve your full potential and achieve life fulfillment.

Joey Yap's Art of Face Reading

The Art of Face Reading is Joey Yap's second effort with CICO Books, and takes a lighter, more practical approach to Face Reading. This book does not so much focus on the individual features as it does on reading the entire face. It is about identifying common personality types and characters.

Easy Guide on Face Reading (English & Chinese versions)

The Face Reading Essentials series of books comprises 5 individual books on the key features of the face – Eyes, Eyebrows, Ears, Nose, and Mouth. Each book provides a detailed illustration and a simple yet descriptive explanation on the individual types of the features.

The books are equally useful and effective for beginners, enthusiasts, and the curious. The series is designed to enable people who are new to Face Reading to make the most of first impressions and learn to apply Face Reading skills to understand the personality and character of friends, family, co-workers, and even business associates.

Annual Releases
2011 Annual Outlook & Tong Shu

Chinese Astrology for 2011 | Feng Shui for 2011 | Tong Shu Desktop Calendar 2011 | Professional Tong Shu Diary 2011 | Tong Shu Monthly Planner 2011 | Weekly Tong Shu Diary 2011

www.masteryacademy.com | +603 - 2284 8080

Educational Tools and Software

Xuan Kong Flying Stars Feng Shui Software
The Essential Application for Enthusiasts and Professionals

The Xuan Kong Flying Stars Feng Shui Software will assist you in the practice of Xuan Kong Feng Shui with minimum fuss and maximum effectiveness. Superimpose the Flying Stars charts over your house plans (or those of your clients) to clearly demarcate the 9 Palaces. Use it to help you create fast and sophisticated chart drawings and presentations, as well as to assist professional practitioners in the report-writing process before presenting the final reports for your clients. Students can use it to practice their Xuan Kong Feng Shui skills and knowledge, and it can even be used by designers and architects!

BaZi Ming Pan Software Version 2.0
Professional Four Pillars Calculator for Destiny Analysis

The BaZi Ming Pan Version 2.0 Professional Four Pillars Calculator for Destiny Analysis is the most technically advanced software of its kind in the world today. It allows even those without any knowledge of BaZi to generate their own BaZi Charts, and provides virtually every detail required to undertake a comprehensive Destiny Analysis.

This Professional Four Pillars Calculator allows you to even undertake a day-to-day analysis of your Destiny. What's more, all BaZi Charts generated by this software are fully printable and configurable! Designed for both enthusiasts and professional practitioners, this state-of-the-art software blends details with simplicity, and is capable of generating 4 different types of BaZi charts: **BaZi Professional Charts, BaZi Annual Analysis Charts, BaZi Pillar Analysis Charts and BaZi Family Relationship Charts.**

Joey Yap Feng Shui Template Set

Directions are the cornerstone of any successful Feng Shui audit or application. The **Joey Yap Feng Shui Template Set** is a set of three templates to simplify the process of taking directions and determining locations and positions, whether it's for a building, a house, or an open area such as a plot of land, all with just a floor plan or area map.

The Set comprises 3 basic templates: The Basic Feng Shui Template, 8 Mansions Feng Shui Template, and the Flying Stars Feng Shui Template.

Mini Feng Shui Compass

The Mini Feng Shui Compass is a self-aligning compass that is not only light at 100gms but also built sturdily to ensure it will be convenient to use anywhere. The rings on the Mini Feng Shui Compass are bi-lingual and incorporate the 24 Mountain Rings that is used in your traditional Luo Pan.

The comprehensive booklet included will guide you in applying the 24 Mountain Directions on your Mini Feng Shui Compass effectively and the 8 Mansions Feng Shui to locate the most auspicious locations within your home, office and surroundings. You can also use the Mini Feng Shui Compass when measuring the direction of your property for the purpose of applying Flying Stars Feng Shui.

Educational Tools and Software

Xuan Kong Vol.1
An Advanced Feng Shui Home Study Course

Learn the Xuan Kong Flying Star Feng Shui system in just 20 lessons! Joey Yap's specialised notes and course work have been written to enable distance learning without compromising on the breadth or quality of the syllabus. Learn at your own pace with the same material students in a live class would use. The most comprehensive distance learning course on Xuan Kong Flying Star Feng Shui in the market. Xuan Kong Flying Star Vol.1 comes complete with a special binder for all your course notes.

Feng Shui for Period 8 - (DVD)

Don't miss the Feng Shui Event of the next 20 years! Catch Joey Yap LIVE and find out just what Period 8 is all about. This DVD boxed set zips you through the fundamentals of Feng Shui and the impact of this important change in the Feng Shui calendar. Joey's entertaining, conversational style walks you through the key changes that Period 8 will bring and how to tap into Wealth Qi and Good Feng Shui for the next 20 years.

Xuan Kong Flying Stars Beginners Workshop - (DVD)

Take a front row seat in Joey Yap's Xuan Kong Flying Stars workshop with this unique LIVE RECORDING of Joey Yap's Xuan Kong Flying Stars Feng Shui workshop, attended by over 500 people. This DVD program provides an effective and quick introduction of Xuan Kong Feng Shui essentials for those who are just starting out in their study of classical Feng Shui. Learn to plot your own Flying Star chart in just 3 hours. Learn 'trade secret' methods, remedies and cures for Flying Stars Feng Shui. This boxed set contains 3 DVDs and 1 workbook with notes and charts for reference.

BaZi Four Pillars of Destiny Beginners Workshop - (DVD)

Ever wondered what Destiny has in store for you? Or curious to know how you can learn more about your personality and inner talents? BaZi or Four Pillars of Destiny is an ancient Chinese science that enables us to understand a person's hidden talent, inner potential, personality, health and wealth luck from just their birth data. This specially compiled DVD set of Joey Yap's BaZi Beginners Workshop provides a thorough and comprehensive introduction to BaZi. Learn how to read your own chart and understand your own luck cycle. This boxed set contains 3 DVDs and 1 workbook with notes and reference charts.

DVD Series

Joey Yap's Face Reading Revealed DVD Series
Mian Xiang, the Chinese art of Face Reading, is an ancient form of physiognomy and entails the use of the face and facial characteristics to evaluate key aspects of a person's life, luck and destiny. In his Face Reading DVDs series, Joey Yap shows you how the facial features reveal a wealth of information about a person's luck, destiny and personality.

Mian Xiang also tell us the talents, quirks and personality of an individual. Do you know that just by looking at a person's face, you can ascertain his or her health, wealth, relationships and career? Let Joey Yap show you how the 12 Palaces can be utilised to reveal a person's inner talents, characteristics and much more.

Feng Shui for Homebuyers DVD Series
In these DVDs, you will also learn how to identify properties with good Feng Shui features that will help you promote a fulfilling life and achieve your full potential. Discover how to avoid properties with negative Feng Shui that can bring about detrimental effects to your health, wealth and relationships.

Joey will also elaborate on how to fix the various aspects of your home that may have an impact on the Feng Shui of your property and give pointers on how to tap into the positive energies to support your goals.

Discover Feng Shui with Joey Yap: Set of 4 DVDs
Informative and entertaining, classical Feng Shui comes alive in *Discover Feng Shui with Joey Yap!*

You have the questions. Now let Joey personally answer them in this 4-set DVD compilation! Learn how to ensure the viability of your residence or workplace, Feng Shui-wise, without having to convert it into a Chinese antiques' shop. Classical Feng Shui is about harnessing the natural power of your environment to improve quality of life. It's a systematic and subtle metaphysical science.

Walking the Dragons with Joey Yap (The TV Series)
This DVD set features eight episodes, covering various landform Feng Shui analyses and applications from Joey Yap as he and his co-hosts travel through China. It includes case studies of both modern and historical sites with a focus on Yin House (burial places) Feng Shui and the tombs of the Qing Dynasty emperors.

The series was partly filmed on-location in mainland China, and the state of Selangor, Malaysia.

www.masteryacademy.com | +603 - 2284 8080

Home Study Courses

Gain Valuable Knowledge from the Comfort of Your Home

Now, armed with your trusty computer or laptop and Internet access, knowledge of Chinese Metaphysics is just a click away!

3 easy steps to activate your Home Study Course:

Step 1:
Go to the URL as indicated on the Activation Card, and key in your Activation Code

Step 2:
At the Registration page, fill in the details accordingly to enable us to generate your Student Identification (Student ID).

Step 3:
Upon successful registration, you may begin your lessons immediately.

Joey Yap's Feng Shui Mastery HomeStudy Course

Module 1: **Empowering Your Home**
Module 2: **Master Practitioner Program**

Learn how easy it is to harness the power of the environment to promote health, wealth and prosperity in your life. The knowledge and applications of Feng Shui will no more be a mystery but a valuable tool you can master on your own.

Joey Yap's BaZi Mastery HomeStudy Course

Module 1: **Mapping Your Life**
Module 2: **Mastering Your Future**

Discover your path of least resistance to success with insights about your personality and capabilities, and what strengths you can tap on to maximize your potential for success and happiness by mastering BaZi (Chinese Astrology). This course will teach you all the essentials you need to interpret a BaZi chart and more.

Joey Yap's Mian Xiang Mastery HomeStudy Course

Module 1: **Face Reading**
Module 2: **Advanced Face Reading**

A face can reveal so much about a person. Now, you can learn the art and science of Mian Xiang (Chinese Face Reading) to understand a person's character based on his or her facial features with ease and confidence.

www.masteryacademy.com | +603 - 2284 8080

Feng Shui Mastery™
LIVE COURSES (MODULES ONE TO FOUR)

The Feng Shui Mastery™ comprises Feng Shui Mastery Modules 1, 2, 3 and 4. It starts off with a foundation program up to the advanced practitioner level. It is a thorough, comprehensive program that covers important theories from various classical Feng Shui systems including Ba Zhai, San Yuan, San He, and Xuan Kong.

Module One: Beginners Course **Module Two:** Practitioners Course **Module Three:** Advanced Practitioners Course **Module Four:** Master Course

BaZi Mastery™
LIVE COURSES (MODULES ONE TO FOUR)

The BaZi Mastery™ consists of BaZi Mastery Modules 1, 2, 3 and 4. In Modules 1 and 2, students will receive a thorough introduction to BaZi, along with an intensive understanding of BaZi principles and the requisite skills to practice it with accuracy and precision. This will prepare them, and serious Feng Shui practitioners, for a more advanced levels and fine-tune their application skills in Modules 3 and 4.

Module One: Intensive Foundation Course **Module Two:** Practitioners Course **Module Three:** Advanced Practitioners Course **Module Four:** Master Course in BaZi

XUAN KONG MASTERY™
LIVE COURSES (MODULES ONE TO THREE)
* Advanced Courses For Master Practitioners

The Xuan Kong Mastery™ comprises Xuan Kong Mastery Modules 1, 2A, 2B and 3. It is a sophisticated branch of Feng Shui replete with many techniques and formulae, enabling practitioners to evaluate Feng Shui on a more thorough and in-depth basis. The study of Xuan Kong encompasses numerology, symbology and science of the Ba Gua along with the mathematics of time.

Module One: Advanced Foundation Course **Module Two A:** Advanced Xuan Kong Methodologies **Module Two B:** Purple White **Module Three:** Advanced Xuan Kong Da Gua

www.masteryacademy.com | +603 - 2284 8080

Mian Xiang Mastery™
LIVE COURSES (MODULES ONE AND TWO)

The Mian Xiang Mastery™ comprises of Mian Xiang Mastery Modules 1 and 2 to allow students to learn this ancient art in a thorough, detailed manner. Each module has a carefully-developed syllabus that allows students to get acquainted with the fundamentals of Mian Xiang before moving on to the more intricate theories and principles that will enable them to practice Mian Xiang with greater depth and complexity.

Module One:
Basic Face Reading

Module Two:
Practical Face Reading

Yi Jing Mastery™
LIVE COURSES (MODULES ONE AND TWO)

The Yi Jing Mastery™ comprises Modules 1 and 2. Both Modules aim to give casual and serious Yi Jing enthusiasts a serious insight into one of the most important philosophical treatises in ancient Chinese thought. Yi Jing uses sophisticated formulas and calculations to derive the answers to questions we pose. It is a science of divination, and in our classes there is a heavy emphasis on the scientific aspect of it. It bears no religious or superstitious affiliation.

Module One:
Traditional Yi Jing

Module Two:
Plum Blossom Numerology

Ze Ri Mastery™
LIVE COURSES (MODULES ONE AND TWO)

The ZeRi Mastery™ consists of ZeRi Mastery Modules 1 and 2. This program provides students with a thorough introduction to the art of Date Selection both for Personal and Feng Shui purposes. Our ZeRi Mastery™ aims to provide a thorough and comprehensive program on the art of Date Selection, covering everything from Personal and Feng Shui Date Selection to Xuan Kong Da Gua Date Selection.

Module One:
Personal and Feng Shui Date Selection

Module Two:
Xuan Kong Da Gua Date Selection

www.masteryacademy.com | +603 - 2284 8080

Feng Shui for Life

This is an entry-level five-day course designed for the Feng Shui beginner to learn the application of practical Feng Shui in day-to-day living. Lessons include quick tips on analyzing the BaZi chart, simple Feng Shui solutions for the home, basic Date Selection, useful Face Reading techniques and practical Water formulas. A great introduction course on Chinese Metaphysics studies for beginners.

Joey Yap's
Design Your Destiny

This is a three-day life transformation program designed to inspire awareness and action for you to create a better quality of life. It introduces the DRT™ (Decision Referential Technology) method, which utilizes the BaZi Personality Profiling system to determine the right version of you, and serves as a tool to help you make better decisions and achieve a better life in the least resistant way possible based on your Personality Profile Type.

Walk the Mountains! Learn Feng Shui in a Practical and Hands-on Program

 ### Feng Shui Mastery Excursion™

Learn landform (Luan Tou) Feng Shui by walking the mountains and chasing the Dragon's vein in China. This Program takes the students in a study tour to examine notable Feng Shui landmarks, mountains, hills, valleys, ancient palaces, famous mansions, houses and tombs in China. The Excursion is a 'practical' hands-on course where students are shown to perform readings using the formulas they've learnt and to recognize and read Feng Shui Landform (Luan Tou) formations.

Read about China Excursion here:
http://www.fengshuiexcursion.com

Mastery Academy courses are conducted around the world. Find out when will Joey Yap be in your area by visiting **www.masteryacademy.com** or call our office at **+603-2284 8080**.